T0293503

ROUTLEDGE LIBRARY EDITIONS:
THE ECONOMICS AND BUSINESS OF
TECHNOLOGY

Volume 31

AN INTRODUCTION TO TECHNOLOGICAL FORECASTING

AN INTRODUCTION TO TECHNOLOGICAL FORECASTING

Edited by
JOSEPH P. MARTINO

Routledge
Taylor & Francis Group

LONDON AND NEW YORK

First published in 1972 by Gordon and Breach Science Publishers, Inc.

This edition first published in 2018
by Routledge
2 Park Square, Milton Park, Abingdon, Oxon OX14 4RN

and by Routledge
711 Third Avenue, New York, NY 10017

Routledge is an imprint of the Taylor & Francis Group, an informa business

British Library Cataloguing in Publication Data
A catalogue record for this book is available from the British Library

ISBN: 978-1-138-50336-6 (Set)
ISBN: 978-1-351-06690-7 (Set) (ebk)
ISBN: 978-0-8153-6487-0 (Volume 31) (hbk)
ISBN: 978-1-351-10645-0 (Volume 31) (ebk)

Publisher's Note
The publisher has gone to great lengths to ensure the quality of this reprint but points out that some imperfections in the original copies may be apparent.

Disclaimer
The publisher has made every effort to trace copyright holders and would welcome correspondence from those they have been unable to trace.

an introduction to

TECHNOLOGICAL FORECASTING

Joseph P. Martino

Editor

GORDON AND BREACH SCIENCE PUBLISHERS

London   Paris   New York

This book is dedicated to Ed Cornish, who thought of it and talked me into doing it, and to Mary, whose quietly effective inspiration and support made it possible.

The Futurist Library

INTRODUCTION

Interest in the future has grown rapidly in recent years, because social
and technological change is occurring so rapidly that it is apparent to
everyone that in as little as 10 or 20 years we will be living in a world
vastly different from the world of today.

Futurists -- the scholars, scientists, government officials, and others who
are seriously interested in the future -- do not claim to know what the
future world will be like. In fact, they generally agree that the future
is fundamentally unknowable because, to be knowable, the future would have
to exist (which it does not, since it has yet to come into being), or else
be predetermined. In either event, futurists would be engaged in a purely
academic axercise, because they could have no influence on the future.

But since the future is neither fixed nor predetermined, man has the
possibility of shaping it. The futurists task is to help him to shape
it more wisely by amplifying his understanding of the choices open to him.
Once he understands the possibilities of the future, he can select those
possible futures that he wishes to make part of the actual future, and can
then bend his efforts to bringing them to reality.

In 1966, a group of people interested in the future founded the World
Future Society: An Association for the Study of Alternative Futures.
The Society was created to serve all those interested in the future --
decision makers in business, education and government, as well as the
forecasters, planners and other experts dealing with the future. Since
its founding, the Society has grown rapidly and today it has thousands of
members in more than 60 nations.

The Society regularly publishes articles dealing with the future in its
journal, The Futurist: A Journal of Forecasts, Trends, and Ideas about the
Future. But limitations of space make it impossible to publish many important
texts within the confines of the Futurist. For this reason, the Society has
launched the World Future Society book series. Each volume in the series
will be a work of exceptional interest to people interested in the future,
and as the series expands it will constitute a library of the future.

The series represents another milestone in the Society's development. These
volumes will hopefully put us in touch with many people whose interest in
the future is now growing but who have not yet made contact with us. Anyone
interested in learning more about the Society and its other activities is
invited to write to me care of the World Future Society, P.O. Box 19285,
Twentieth Street Station, Washington D.C. 20036. I will be most happy
to send him information and a membership application.

Edward S. Cornish, President
World Future Society

PREFACE

"Technological forecasting is a new and rapidly growing subject of great importance," says the technological forecaster. But wait a minute, the skeptic says. Important? Only time will tell. Growing? Possibly. But new? Surely not. What about Arthur C. Clarke? Robert A. Heinlein? H.G. Wells? Jules Verne? Leonardo da Vinci? Weren't they doing technological forecasting, some of them quite a long time ago?

It is quite true that writers of science fiction and of serious speculation, as well as scientists turned philosopher, have for centuries been making predictions about future technological developments. However, the recent upsurge in technological forecasting differs from this earlier work in two important respects. First, it is being done by people solidly in the main stream of current scientific thought, as part of their contribution to that main stream. It is not being done by people on the periphery of science, or by scientists temporarily taking up the role of forecaster. Second, it is being done in a conscious and deliberate attempt to influence the policies and decisions of government and business executives with regard to science and technology.

Technological forecasting, with these two distinguishing characteristics, is just a little over a decade old. Ralph Lenz's pioneering work, as reported in his Masters Thesis, was published in 1959. Even Lenz's publication of a technical report at Wright Field, in 1962, did not immediately generate any significant response. It was only in the late 1960's, with a sudden increase of interest in the problem of planning and controlling the mushrooming growth of research and development, that widespread interest in technological forecasting came about. Perhaps the milestone event, signifying the existence of an already rapidly rising trend, was the publication of *Technological Forecasting in Perspective*, written by Erich Jantsch for the OECD. This massive survey uncovered far more activity in the field than anyone had realized existed. Since its publication in 1967, this work was followed by a flood of articles, books and conferences, devoted to the topic of technological forecasting. Even so, the subject is so new that the *Readers Guide to Periodical Literature*, the *Engineering Index*, and the *Applied Science and Technology Index*, three of the best references to the technical periodical literature, have not yet recognized technological forecasting as a subject to be indexed separately. In all three references, articles on technological forecasting are indexed in many different places. Thus technological forecasting, in the sense described above, is both new and rapidly growing.

But wait again, the skeptic says. If there is such a flood of material coming on the market, why this book? Why add one more publication to a total which is already too big for anyone to read completely? I believe this book fills a unique spot in the literature. Virtually all the existing books fall into either of two categories. On the one hand, there are highly technical works which give detailed descriptions of how to make technological forecasts. On the other hand, there are works of a popular nature, intended either to entertain or awe the reader with descriptions of the technology of tomorrow. This book does not attempt to do either. It does not present any forecasts simply for the sake of entertainment. Nor does it give sufficient information for anyone not previously familiar with the subject to begin making professional-quality forecasts. Instead, this book is intended for the serious reader who wants to know about technological forecasting, but not necessarily how to do it himself. What is technological forecasting? What is it good for? How can it be used? These are the questions this book attempts to answer. And these are the questions which should be asked by the business executive, the government official, the social critic, and the interested citizen, who wants to know what technological forecasting means to him.

In addition, this book has another purpose. Much of the existing work, especially the popularized treatments of technological forecasting, have an air of "Here comes the future; get with it or you'll get run over!" The writers take the attitude that the future is up there ahead of us, perhaps just around the bend, and whether we like it or not, we'd better get used to it. If there is one common thread among the essays in this book, it is the negation of this idea of the inevitability of a particular future. The future is not up there waiting for us; the future will be what we make it. To a greater extent, we do have a choice about the kind of future we will have. Technological forecasting is a tool to help us make that choice in an intelligent manner. Thus the technological forecaster is also right in claiming that his work is important. It is important not only to him, but to the decision maker in business or government, and to the citizen at large. In a democracy, where ultimately the choices made reflect the desires of the citizenry, it is essential that the citizenry know what the choices are; what the options open to them are. This book is intended to tell the decision maker and the interested citizen about technological forecasting, and its role in informing them of the choices they will have to make.

The kind permission of the following copyright holders, for use of certain essays in this book, is acknowledged. *Air University Review*, for permission to reprint my own article, "Forecasting the Progress of Technology," which appeared in the March-April 1969 issue, Vol XX, No. 3. Batelle Memorial Institute and *The Engineering Economist*, for "Industrial Implications of Technological Forecasting," presented at the Fourth Summer Symposium of the Engineering Economy Division, American Society for Engineering Education, June 19 - 20, 1965. MIT Press, for "The Triumph of Technology: 'Can' Implies 'Ought'", which appeared in *Planning for Diversity and Choice*, edited by Stanford Anderson, and published by MIT Press. The Cape Canaveral Section of the American Institute of Aeronautics and Astronautics for "Technological Forecasting and Space Exploration," which appeared in *Q.E.D.*, the Section magazine, for October 1966.

TABLE OF CONTENTS

What is the philosophical basis behind technological forecasting? In
what way does it differ from any
other kind of forecasting? Can it
really claim to be a science, or to
have a scientific basis? These are
some of the questions Mr. Hacke addresses in the following essay.

A METHODOLOGICAL PREFACE TO TECHNOLOGICAL FORECASTING

JAMES E. HACKE, JR.*

Stanford Research Institute, Menlo Park, Cal., U.S.A.

ABSTRACT

To regard induction as less dependable or "logical" than deduction
is a fallacy. Only when empirical, inductive methods were applied to
natural phenomena did a powerful body of natural science develop. Empirical science is subject to some ambiguities and limitations; but they
are characteristic of all human thought. Three unique elements in the
methods of empirical science give it its power: the deliberate design of
experiments seeking to disprove a hypothesis; the systematic assessment
and measurement of precision; and the erection of a general body of theory "explaining" particular facts and laws.

The success of empirical science has led to adaptation of its methods
in a variety of disciplines, despite objections that these methods were
inappropriate in these disciplines. Although scientific statements have
in themselves a predictive connotation, use of scientific facts and laws
for prediction is most conspicuous in such arts as medicine and engineering.

Forecasting shares many of the limitations and ambiguities of empirical science, and many of the objections raised to forecasting stem from
these limitations and ambiguities. To some extent, the forecaster may be
able to adapt the testing of hypotheses, the measurement of precision, and
the erection of general theories that have made empirical science so powerful. As empirical science has moved from the relatively tractable to the
relatively intractable, despite objections, so has forecasting. But forecasting is not a science in itself; it is an art like medicine or engineering. Like these arts, it draws most of its facts and laws from the empirical sciences.

INTRODUCTION

This paper is an attempt to state concisely and precisely some necessary methodological antecedents to the task of forecasting technological
change. In another age or culture, our starting point might have been
different: Aristotelian metaphysics in the Middle Ages, or the Hegelian
dialect in the Soviet Union. Here and now, however, we can hardly start
with anything other than the methods of empirical science.

---

*This paper was presented at the first Symposium on Long Range Fore-
casting and Planning, held at the Air Force Academy, August 16 - 17,
1966, Colorado Springs, Colorado, U.S.A.

Section II, therefore, is a methodological consideration of empirical science. It sets forth some of its limitations and ambiguities, and seeks to show why empirical science is nevertheless our most powerful tool for learning about the phenomenal universe. We apply the findings of empirical science for their predictive value in such fields as medicine or engineering.

Section III is a methodological consideration of forecasting. It shows the close parallel between the methods of empirical science and those of forecasting, and suggests that, as science shares some of the limitations and ambiguities for which forecasting is faulted, perhaps forecasting can share some of the more powerful elements in scientific method. Forecasting is, indeed, an application of the findings of empirical science just as medicine and engineering are.

The concluding Section IV draws some inferences from these methodological considerations for the task of the technological forecaster today.

This section contains an exposition in five parts:

A. Natural science became powerful only when it adopted empirical, inductive methods.

B. These methods entail some important limitations and ambiguities.

C. But the methods of empirical science embrace other elements that assure its power.

D. The methods of empirical science have been adapted to fields of study in which some at first thought them not applicable.

E. The results of empirical science are useful for prediction, especially in medicine and engineering.

A.   *Induction and Deduction*

Most of us tend to assume, without fully realizing it, that deduction is somehow more "logical" than induction, particularly the kind of induction known as empirical inference. In fact, the deductive syllogism itself is an axiom arrived at by empirical inference, and is as much a description of the way we think as it is a rule for being logical.

The deductive syllogism has the status of an axiom in formal logic. This is the same status that the parallel postulate has in Euclidian geometry. Euclid regarded his axioms as self-evident truths; but we have come to be distrustful of self-evident truths! Indeed, if Eistein's Theory of General Relativity be true, the parallel postulate is neither self-evident nor so.

The most we can say about the deductive syllogism as an axiom of logic is that it leads to no logical inconsistencies. Lewis Carroll wrote a delightful fable [1] demonstrating that, if an individual refuses to accept the validity of a syllogism, one cannot force him to.

As a habit of thought, the deductive syllogism is the way we tend to state propositions that we have arrived at empirically. Take, for instance, the old exemplar syllogism: "All men are mortal; Socrates is a man; Socrates is mortal." If this be regarded as a statement of fact, its meaning is this: We are in the habit of classifying all objects as either human or not human. The object named Socrates offers every evidence of

being human. We therefore attribute mortality to Socrates, too. If he
were to remain alive for an unreasonably long time, we are likely to say,
"He cannot be a *mere* man!" We tend to put exceptions to the rule into
special categories - Man-with-a-Difference - in order to keep the syl-
logisms inviolate.

So impressed were natural philosophers from Aristotle to Descartes
with the power of syllogistic logic that they tried to derive the laws of
nature from general principles conceived of as self-evident. In short,
they tried to make physical science a deductive system like syllogistic
logic or Euclidian geometry. But we can arrive at "self-evident" principles in science, or in anything else, only by intuitive induction! Not
surprisingly, therefore, when natural scientists, beginning with Sir
Francis Bacon, began self-consciously to use induction in order to discover the general principles of science, they triumphed rapidly over deductive natural philosophy.

B. *Limitations and Ambiguities*

Being empirical and inductive, natural science is subject to some
important limitations and ambiguities. In reality, it shares these with
all human thought; but they are especially important to an understanding
of scientific method.

1. The scientist has no more warrant than the rest of us for claiming that because events have hitherto occurred in a certain pattern they
will continue to do so. No more; but, also, no less. The scientist is
in the same predicament as the rest of us: he has no *proof* that the past
is a guide to the future; but unless he *assumes* it, he can do nothing.
He starts with the same naive realism with which we all start; but he
goes on to investigate as precisely as he can the relation between a
statement like "The sun has risen every day so far" and statements like
"The sun will rise tomorrow." In the process, he gets involved with inverse probabilities and attempts like Bayes' Theorem [2] to assess the
likelihood of a future event on the basis of past experience.

2. Empirical methods will work at all only to the extent that the
laws of nature are in fact capable of being expressed in a form independent of location and time. There was some speculation, a few years ago,
that the value of the velocity of light in a vacuum is a slowly-fluctuat-
ing function of time. If it were, we should never be able to detect it
except by comparing it with something *assumed* unvarying with time. For
another example: A really unique event would remain forever inexplicable
as far as natural science is concerned. Others might call it a miracle
or a fortuitous combination of circumstances, but science could never
say.

3. The scientist begins his search for regularity in his environment where we all do: with the most obvious and compelling of his ex-
periences. Through a continual exploration and refinement, he reaches
far beyond the immediate data to the unsensed and the insensible. There
is no *a priori* guarantee that his view of reality thus achieved is independent of his starting place. The scientist must take it on faith
that his science is not overly distorted by his starting point, or by his
subsequent decisions about what to study.

4. Similarly, the scientist must take it on faith that his view of
reality is not overly distorted by his peculiar modes of thinking. We
have, for example, a great propensity for adducing patterns where none in
fact exist. Think of the constellations: people, beasts, and other terrestrial objects "seen" by men of old in the stars. How much of our body

of "scientific" knowledge consists of patterns adduced where non in fact
exist?

5. The regularities that natural science discovers are approximate
both in form and in the precision with which their parameters are known.
One of the most precisely verified laws of science is the inverse-square
law of electrostatic attraction or repulsion. If, in fact, the force between two charged bodies varies precisely with the inverse of the square
of their distance apart, then the field inside a charged hollow conductor
must be precisely zero. This result has been verified at least as accurately as one part in a billion, by graduate assistants working inside
the globes of Van de Graaf machines charged to a million volts as well as
in other ways. But it has been verified only for charged bodies within
a finite range of size, and within a finite range of gravitational fields.
What about a charged body the size of the Milky Way out in intergalactic
space?

6. Almost tautologically, the goal of empirical science is to replace brute facts with general laws. We have steam tables because water
vapor is not a perfect gas; but the scientist is much happier with the
situation obtaining with perfect gases. For them, he can substitute Van
der Waal's equation for all the tabulated data. Heaven, for the scientist,
would be the state of blessedness in which everything is explicable in
terms of a Most General Possible Law and of a Single Initial Fact. Everything else, including the scientist's own name, address, and telephone
number, would be deducible from that Fact in terms of that Law.

In this imperfect world, however, we have things like the Fine-
Structure Constant. That constant is close to 1/137. It is because it
is, as far as we know; and that is why it is. This is such an unsatisfac-
tory condition for the scientist that he is forced to an act of faith:
Some day scientists will know why it is 1/137 and not, say, 1/138.

7. As you know, scientists are supposed to use Occam's Razor to
"shave" their hypotheses down to the minimum possible, and the simplest
possible, and still account adequately for the facts. One could claim for
instance, that when God created the universe in 4004 B.C., he created it
complete with fossils to mislead infidel scientists; but Occam's Razor
renders this an unscientific hypothesis.

Yet the problem of deciding which of two hypotheses is the simpler
is not always trivial. Often there is an element of elegance, of symmetry, of appropriateness that leads a scientist to choose a novel approach to a problem. Conversely, it is an intuitive sense of inappropri-
ateness that makes physicists unhappy with a fine structure constant of
1/137. The numbers 1, 1/2, 2, 3, or even ε or π, alone or in combination,
might be considered appropriate; but not the reciprocal of a large prime
number.

The principle of symmetry has been called "the principle of minimum
astonishment." Physical theory makes great use of this principle; and
it is full of pitfalls for the unwary. Indeed, as the overthrow of parity
shows, our most eminent scientists can misapply it. It is really nothing
more than an appeal to the individual's intuitive sense of the fitness of
things.

8. A scientific law can be disproved; but it can never be proved.
A single instance in which the law fails disproves it; but no number of
instances in which it works will prove it. Such instances merely confirm
it: that is, make firmer.

For example, Bode's Rule gives the radii of the planetary orbits in astronomical units: Add 4 to the sequence 0, 3, 6, 12, 24, 48, ..., and divide by 10. At first there was no known planet to occupy the fifth place in this series; then the asteroids were discovered. After the rule was formulated, Uranus and Neptune were discovered; their orbits fell acceptably near the predictions of Bode's Rule. By then, the rule seemed well confirmed! But then Pluto was discovered, and Pluto's orbit is not even within hailing distance of the prediction of Bode's Rule. Bode's Rule went to the graveyard of physical theories: It became a rule of thumb.

C. *Strengthening Elements of Scientific Method*

In spite of these limitations, empirical science is as powerful as it is largely because of the following three characteristics of its method:

1. Scientific method consists not only in formulating hunches about regularities observed in nature. It consists also in putting these hunches to the test [3]. The experimenter devises as many ways as he can of *disproving* his hunch. If none works, the hunch is to some degree confirmed. As that confirmation becomes more and more impressive, the hunch receives progressively more dignified names: hypothesis; theory; law.

2. The scientist measures, and accounts for, the errors in his measurements. If his results do not agree with expectations, within a range of values determined by measurements of precision, there is a discrepancy to be accounted for. This assessment of error serves both to measure how confident the scientist may be in the precision of his measurements, and also as an objective test of whether or not a hypothesis is confirmed.

3. The scientist is not content merely to express observed relationships in an empirical law. He seeks also to relate empirical laws to one another through a general theory. These theories usually involve assumed entities, such as molecules, fields, vibrations, and quanta, that are not logically demanded by the facts [4].

Take the laws of a perfect gas, for example. As long as this law remains in the form "PV = MRT," it expresses an entirely empirical relationship. But when we invoke molecules in motion, impinging on one another and on the walls of the container, we are out of the realm of empirical relationships and in the realm of the kinetic theory of gases. We have established a relationship between billiards and the behavior of gases. And we are left with molecules that have more "thinglike" qualities than the general gas law really demands. We use the excess properties in "explaining" acoustics, gaseous viscosity, and Brownian movement. All these phenomena, including the general gas laws, are "explained" only in the sense that they are exhibited as consequences derivable from a general theory. Indeed, that is the only kind of scientific "explanation" there is.

These elements of the scientific method continually interact. A new hunch suggests a relationship between two classes of phenomena not previously seen to be related. The scientist devises ways of putting his hunch to the test. His experimental results suggest new hunches to him. Through such interactions, the powerful and largely unified body of consistent scientific theory has grown. In the process, many empirical laws received two kinds of accreditation: events so far have confirmed them in practice; and they have been "explained" as one consequence of a large and unified body of theory.

But this "explanation" in terms of scientific theory is not essential to the trustworthiness of a scientific fact. We still do not know why aspirin dulls pain. Benjamin Franklin had to "decide" which way electricity "flows" a hundred years before discovery of the electron. Most of us were raised on the platitude that we do not know what electricity is, we just know how to use it. Even today, we "know" what electricity "is" only in the sense that we can "explain" it in terms of more general atomic theory.

D. *Expanding Applicability of Empirical Methods*

Empirical methods were first applied in physics and chemistry. In these disciplines, the phenomena to be studied were relatively accessible to experiment and, initially at least, relatively simple. As their methods became progressively confirmed by experience, scientists applied them to the extent possible in astronomy, geology, biology, psychology, sociology, economics, anthropology, and archeology. With regard to each of these fields, people objected that the methods of empirical science could not be applied or would not work, for one or more of the following reasons:

1. The phenomena of the field embody some transcendental factor not amenable to the laws of science: the "vital principle" in biology or the "soul" in psychology.

2. The phenomena of the field are too complex to yield to quantitative analysis.

3. Practical or ethical considerations prevent experimentation, especially in some areas of medicine and behavioral sciences.

4. Because of temporal or spatial distances, the phenomena of the field are inaccessible to direct experimentation: astronomy, geology, and archeology.

5. The subjects being studied are rational, selfconscious beings, and thus deliberately or inadvertently act abnormally under observation. In particular, awareness of psychological, sociological, or anthropological findings can "poison" experimental data in these fields.

In each of these fields, however, these objections have at least partially been overcome. In most, statistical analysis and demonstration of consistency with the rest of the body of scientific knowledge have borne the burden of dealing with complexity and inaccessibility. Only regarding cosmological speculation is there real doubt that conclusions are "scientific" in any empirical sense [5].

E. *Empirical Science and Prediction*

Although the scientist may try to deny it, scientific laws have a predictive connotation even within the bosom of "pure" science. Unless he be forewarned, the scientist is likely to state Newton's first law like this: "A body at rest will remain at rest, and a body in motion will remain in uniform motion, unless acted on by an external force." Forewarned, he may cast it in the conditional: "*If* a body is at rest, it will remain at rest; and *if* a body is in motion, it will remain in uniform motion, *unless* acted on by an external force." But in the real world there are bodies at rest with one another, and there are bodies in relative motion with respect to one another; and of these bodies the conditional statement has all the effect of a prediction.

This application of the laws of science to an actual situation is, of course, at the heart of technology; and it is here that the predictive

quality of scientific laws rules supreme. If I did not have implicit confidence in the predictive accuracy of the laws of physics, as applied in
civil and aeronautical engineering, I should have had to trust in magic
to keep the trains on the track and the planes in the air long enough to
get me here!

METHODOLOGICAL STATUS OF FORECASTING

This section follows an outline precisely parallel to the previous
one:

A. Forecasting shares the empirical, inductive character of natural
science.

B. This character entails some important limitations and ambiguities. Forecasting is therefore faulted for characteristics it shares
with empirical science.

C. Forecasting may also be able to share in the characteristics of
empirical science that give it power.

D. Forecasting has been applied to fields of study which some at
first considered not susceptible to forecast.

E. Forecasting is not itself a science, but, like medicine and engineering, an art applying the results of science.

A. *The Inductive Character of Forecasting*

As in natural science, there have been attempts to derive forecasting
principles from a few "self-evident" axioms. In my opinion, the notion
that there are any "self-evident" axioms is illusory. We arrive at them
by empirical inference, as we arrive at any generalization. A more powerful art of forecasting should develop from recognizing the essentially inductive character of all our knowledge and by applying to forecasting the
empirical, inductive methods developed in the natural sciences.

As we shall see, forecasting shares in all of the limitations and
ambiguities incumbent on empirical science. It might as well share in
some of its strengths.

B. *Limitations and Ambiguities*

Many of the ambiguities and limitations for which forecasting is
faulted result from its empirical, inferential character. But these are
characteristics that it shares not only with empirical science but also,
in recognized or unrecognized fact, with all reasoning. The following
list precisely parallels that in Section II, Part B:

1. All prediction, from engineering application of the laws of science on through the writing of alternative *futuribles* [6] or scenarios of
the future, rest on the assumption that the future is going to be like
the past, only more so. The alternative methods of forecasting, outlined by Lenz, [7] Bell, [8] and others, necessarily share this assumption.
They differ only in what they assume will remain constant, under the mul-
tifarious phenomenal changes, and in how they arrive at and apply these
constancies.

2. Forecasting will work only to the extent that the general principles underlying phenomena do not change with time. Forecasting differs
from physical science in that this constraint is by no means merely

speculative. So many of the parameters characterizing the human predicament are traversing entirely novel ranges of value in these days that we
should expect entirely new cross-couplings and nonlinearities to put in
their appearance. To name but two examples:

(a) The carbon-dioxide concentration in the earth's atmosphere is
significantly increasing from all the fossil-fuel burning that we do. The
earth is therefore retaining more of the heat that it receives from the
sun, so its mean temperature is becoming measurably warmer. As our plans
for supersonic-transports and flying buses carrying 500 passengers or
more indicate, this trend is likely to continue, in spite of the increasing use of atomic fuels.

(b) A species of swan in the British Isles maintains a relatively
constant population, because its nesting area is quite circumscribed.
When it gets too crowded, they do not breed. Is it conceivable that
human beings might react in some analogous way, if the earth gets too
crowded, before plague, pestilence, famine, and war take over the regu-
lation of human population?

3. The forecaster like the scientist begins in the middle of things,
and forecasts what seems most obvious and compelling to him. As he works
progressively to refine and improve his forecasts, he can only take it on
faith that his starting point, and his choices along the way, will not too
much distort the projection of reality that he eventually achieves.

4. The forecaster like the scientist has prescientific habits of
thought, and can only hope that they do not too much color the forecasts
he makes. He knows, for instance, that apparently cyclic phenomena have
a hypnotic effect on the human mind. He will therefore distrust forecasts based on harmonic analysis of anything from the sunspot cycle to
the business cycle, unless there are compelling theoretical grounds for
suspecting that a causal relation underlies the apparent relationship.

5. The regularities that the forecaster discovers, like those of the
empirical scientist, are necessarily approximate in form as well as in
parameters. Failure to recognize this fact lies behind two kinds of ab-
surdities: the kind exemplified by the forecast that the human population
will become infinite in a finite number of years; and the kind exemplified by complex models of technological progress with all relationships
linear. Many curves are linear over a restricted range. If the forecaster has no *a priori* grounds for expecting a particular type of relationship, he would be safest in restricting himself to a period, and a
range of dependent variables, commensurate with those in the period for
which he has historical data.

6. Almost tautologically, the goal of forecasting is to replace intuitive hunches with a set of general, interrelated principles of forecasting. I do not mean, of course, that we expect forecasting to become
as determinate and accurate as, say, electrostatic theory. In my
opinion, we shall always have our fine-structure constants, our inexplicable brute facts, in forecasting; and we shall always have unforeseen
events, such as the assassination of President Kennedy, that play hob with
our forecasts. But we can express the hope that forecasting, including
technological forecasting, will become possible over useful time spans,
within preassigned confidence limits, and subject to revision if pre-
specified events occur.

7. In the process of organizing and refining the art of forecasting,
we hope progressively to reduce the element of private judgment and to
increase the element of empirical law involved in the forecasts. To the
extent that the laws are empirical, they are capable of confirmation or

disproof by experiment or experience. But the choice among formulations of laws that explain the data equally well will always rest on the fore-caster's sense of the fitness of things.

For some time to come, we may have to rely largely on this intuitive sense in deciding whether to extrapolate present growth curves, to in-vestigate current trends in birth and death rates and their effects on the population profile, or to correlate, say, birth rates with income and international tension and death rates with expenditures on medical re-search. As we develop a general body of forecasting theory, these in-tuitive choices will recede from the actual forecasting task to the higher reaches of theory; but they will always be present somewhere in the sys-tem.

8. A principle of forecasting can be disproved; but it can never be proved. It can be "explained," that is, exhibited as an instance of a more general law; and it can be "confirmed," that is, known to apply in more and yet more instances; but it can never be "proved" as a theorem in geometry is proved.

In my opinion, much of the extant skepticism about the usefulness of forecasting rests on failure to recognize these distinctions. For example, Schoeffler's book [9] is extremely important to the methodology of forecasting. For one thing, it is replete with examples of forecasts that failed, and thereby disproved something in the hypothetical formu-lations underlying them. But his methodological criticism of these formulations rests almost entirely on their being the same kinds of sim-plification, generalization, and isolation of variables used in the phy-sical sciences. He calls them "unwarranted" or "artificial"; in my opinion, the major justification for these epithets is that the methods failed to produce accurate forecasts.

C. *Strengthening Elements of Forecasting Methods*

The three unique characteristics of scientific method, that probably have most to do with its power, are applicable to forecasting:

1. The forecaster can start by formulating testable hypotheses about the forces underlying the trends he sees, and then devise ways of testing these hypotheses by trying to disprove them. One way of doing this is by applying assumed principles to earlier years in history and then seeing if the principles are capable of "forecasting" conditions in later years. Two studies now under way at the Institute have objectives somewhat of this nature:

(a) We are analyzing forecasts and treatises on forecasting for the Institute's Long Range Planning Service, in order to classify the fore-casting methods used or discussed and the assumptions underlying them. Forecasts that are old enough can be checked against how things turned out. In this way, we may be able to confirm some hypotheses about fore-casting, and disprove others.

(b) We are trying to asses for the National Science Foundation the feasibility of anticipating the economic and social consequences of a major technological innovation, such as the laser. If we come to the con-clusion that anticipating such consequences is indeed feasible under suitable conditions, we shall pick a historical innovation, such as the transistor, and go back to the data available at some fixed time, say 1950. Using these data, we shall try to "forecast" the economic and so-cial consequences up through the present. Then we shall compare the prediction with the actuality. Needless to say, such after-the-fact "forecasting" is open to all sorts of chicanery; but we shall try to be honest.

2.   Technological forecasting needs a precision apparatus, for two purposes: to give the user of the forecast some indication of how accurate the forecaster thinks he is; and to give an objective indication of when the forecast is wrong, so that the forecaster can improve his methods. Failure to give expected error limits, and stating quantitative forecasts with too great an apparent precision, detract from rather than add to the credibility of forecasts.

3.   Forecasting could benefit from a unified body of theory "explaining" particular forecasting methods and trends. In my opinion, however, forecasters have been too prone to the sweeping generalization and the "self-evident truth." The empirical relationship and the statistical correlation of variables have as much place in forecasting as in empirical science. It might be possible to erect some general principles of forecasting on relationships so perceived, and on the laws of science; but these general principles should be arrived at by induction and tested at each step.

D.   *Expanding Scope of Forecasting*

Forecasting began with the magical rites of primitive religion; but so did science, medicine, and the arts. The first self-conscious attempt to forecast on the basis of observed regularities in the natural order of which I am aware is the Egyptians correlating of the flood season of the Nile with the rising of the star Syrius at sunrise [10]. Forecasting of seed time and harvest time, and short-range forecasting of the weather, were undoubtedly the first forecasts put to widespread practical use.

As forecasting has become progressively more dependable and more necessary, it has been applied successively in demography, economics, sociology, ideology, and technology. At each step of the way, it has been opposed on one or more of the following grounds:

1.   The phenomena of the field embody some transcendental factor not amenable to the laws of science: human freedom and unpredictability, or the essentially unpredictable quality of creative innovation.

2.   The phenomena in the field are too complex to yield to quantitative analysis.

3.   Practical or ethical considerations prevent experimental verification.

4.   The phenomena of the field are inaccessible, being in the future; and the success or failure of *past* forecasts says little about prospects for present forecasts: they build on new and unrepeatable conditions.

5.   The subjects being investigated are rational, self-conscious beings, and thus deliberately or inadvertently act abnormally under observation. Forecasts alter the future they forecast; otherwise, there would be little point in making them.

But these are precisely the same objections that accompanied attempts to extend the methods of empirical science into cosmological, biological, and behavioral areas. It follows that these objections are not in themselves disabling, but function rather as cautions to the forecaster in developing and assessing his methods.

E. *Forecasting and Empirical Science*

Methodologically, empirical science and forecasting share many characteristics; but this fact does not make of forecasting a science in itself.
Engineering and other technical arts such as medicine also share many
methodological characteristics with empirical science. The difference
between empirical science, on the one hand, and arts such as engineering,
medicine, and forecasting, on the other, is not so much in method as in
purpose. Science seeks to understand; engineering, medicine, and forecasting seek to apply this understanding to the solution of human problems.

Like other applications of science, forecasting develops its own
techniques and procedures, and its own pragmatic rules. But we should
expect eventually to demonstrate that these techniques, procedures, and
rules are consequences of principles discovered in the physical and social sciences.

CONCLUSIONS

A. Perhaps we have worried too much about the legitimacy of forecasting,
and too little about making forecasting legitimate. This paper hopefully
contributes to the demonstration that forecasting can be methodologically
as legitimate as other applications of empirical science. In any event,
we must forecast; the complexity, power, and rapid change of our environment demands it. If we devote our energies primarily to evaluating,
criticizing, and refining our methods, we may have some chance of keeping
up with the accelerating pace of things with forecasts timely enough, and
accurate enough, to be useful.

B. Forecasting methods by and large have "just growed," like Topsy. We
are now in the process of investigating, methodologically and pragmatically, the status and performance of all forecasting methods we can discover; and we hope that this will serve to advance the development of a
complete and adequate set of forecasting tools. In my opinion, the
danger now is of premature closure: of assuming too quickly that some
methods are more "quantitative" or "objective" or "rigorous" than others,
and therefore more dependable. There may be little assurance, for instance, that the Delphi technique, or any other pooling of the opinions
of experts, will converge, or that if they do converge it will be to what
the future will bring; but there may be just as little warrant for assuming that the trend exhibited by a "well-behaved" curve representing
an isolated phenomenon will continue unperturbed by novel events. Consider, for example, the birth-rate curves of the U.S.A. between 1900 and
1940.

C. As the methods of technological forecasting increase in power and
precision, we shall have to take more seriously, rather than less, the uncertainty that must characterize our forecasts. This uncertainty does
not necessarily result from any lack of determinism in our environment.
It results rather from the inaccuracy of our knowledge of our environment;
and it also results from the impact that our forecasts may have on the
reality they forecast. As forecasts become more precise, they are more
likely to be believed; and belief is likely to lead to modification in
courses of action. The forecaster must therefore take into account the
effect of the forecast itself on the thing forecast. There would undoubtedly be some behavioral analog of the Heisenberg uncertainty relation operating here to keep one from anticipating with complete

accuracy what this impact of the forecast itself will be.

The measurement of precision suggested in the previous conclusion would enable the forecaster to take this uncertainty into account. Indeed, it is only when the forecaster tries to state the precision of his forecast that he need worry about uncertainty. The probabilistic forecast, with the uncertainties stated and the inaccuracies estimated, most closely corresponds with the methods of empirical science, and so yields the maximally trustworthy portrayal of the future.

REFERENCES

1.   CARROLL, L., What the Tortoise Said to Achilles and Other Riddles, reprinted in James R. Newman, ed., *The World of Mathematics*, pp. 2402 ff. New York, Simon and Schuster, 1956.

2.   Cf. TRICKER, R.A.R., *The Assessment of Scientific Speculation*, pp. 39 ff. New York, American Elsevier Publishing Company, Inc., 1965.

3.   Cf. PLATT, J.R., Strong Inference, *Science*, *146*, 3642, pp. 347 ff. October, 1964.

4.   Cf. CARNAP, R., Testability and Meaning, especially pp. 81 ff. H. Feigl and M. Brodbeck, eds., In: *Readings in the Philosophy of Science*, New York, Appleton-Century-Crofts, Inc., 1953.

5.   Cf. BRIDGEMANN, P.W., *The Nature of Physical Theory*, pp. 109 ff. New York, Dover Publications, 1936.

6.   De JUVENAL, B., Futuribles, Santa Monica, RAND Corporation, *Report P-3045*, January 1965.

7.   LENZ, R.C. Jr., *Technological Forecasting*, 2nd ed. Wright-Patterson AFT, Ohio, *Report No. ASD-TDR-62-414*, January 1962.

8.   BELL, D., Twelve Modes of Prediction, J. Gould, ed., In: *Penguin Survey of the Social Sciences*, pp. 96 ff. New York, Penguin Books, 1965.

9.   SCHOEFFLER, S., *The Failures of Economics: a Diagnostic Study*, Cambridge, Harvard University Press, 1955.

10. *Encyclopaedia Britannica*, *4*, 575, 1949.

How is technological forecasting
to be done? How can the scientific
underpinnings, described by Mr.
Hacke, be used to prepare an actual
forecast? The following essay gives
a quick overview of the currently
available methods for producing
technological forecasts.

FORECASTING THE PROGRESS OF TECHNOLOGY*

Lt. Col. JOSEPH P. MARTINO

United States Air Force

The very nature of the Air Force is strongly influenced by technology. Not only the equipment it uses but also its organization, the
skills needed by its members, and the physical facilities it must have
depened upon available technology. Likewise, the Air Force of the future
will be influenced strongly by the technology available then. Actions
which affect the Air Force of the future, including the recruiting of
personnel, the training given new personnel, and decisions about new construction, must take into account future technological developments. How
can the planner determine what the technology of the future will be like,
so that he can take account of it in his plans and decisions? This involves an art and science known as "technological forecasting". Just
what is technological forecasting? And how is it done?

In a sense, technological forecasting has been going on for centuries. Flying machines, long-distance communications, sound-recording
apparatus, and so on have been discussed speculatively by many thinkers.
Bacon and Da Vinci are only two of the great names associated with speculation of this kind. Since the beginning of the Industrial Revolution,
writers of fiction have frequently made forecasts of advanced technology,
as a vehicle for the story they wanted to write. In what way, then, does
modern technological forecasting differ from such speculations?

Ralph Lenz, one of the pioneers of technological forecasting within
the Air Force, has described it as follows:

Technological forecasting may be defined as the prediction of the
invention, characteristics, dimensions, or performance of a machine
serving some useful purpose. ... The qualities sought for the methods
of prediction are explicitness, quantitative expression, reproducibi-
lity of results, and derivation on a logical basis.

The difference between technological forecasting and speculation,
then, lie primarily in the attempts of the forecaster to achieve precision in the description of the useful machine who characteristics he is
forecasting and in his attempts to place the forecast on a sound scientific foundation through the use of logical and explicit methods. A
well-done forecast will state the predicted characteristics of the machine being forecast and make clear the means by which the forecast was
arrived at.

*Reprinted from: *Air University Review*, *20*, 3, March-April, 1969.

However, the forecast of a future invention must be distinguished from the act of invention itself. A forecast may predict levels of performance that are well beyond the current state of the art; it may even predict levels of performance that exceed the theoretical or physical limits of currently used devices or machines. The forecast will not specify how these limitations are to be overcome; it will state only that by a certain time in the future the limitations will have been overcome by means as yet unknown, possibly including the invention of a new device not subject to the limitations of current devices. In short, a forecast predicts that an invention will have been made but does not do the inventing.

How is it possible to forecast the detailed characteristics of future machines, especially when these machines may rely on inventions and discoveries not yet made? A wide variety of methods is in use for making these forecasts, five of which will be described. These are intuitive forecasts, consensus methods, analogy, trend extrapolation, and structural models.

INTUITIVE FORECASTS

Intuitive forecasting is almost certainly the most widely used method. It is the kind of forecast obtained by "asking an expert". The assumption behind the use of this method is that the expert in some field of technology has a broad background of knowledge and experience upon which he can draw to forecast where his field is going. However, the record shows that the experts have been far from infallible. Arthur C. Clarke, in *Profiles of the Future*, describes some famous negative predictions, made by unquestioned authorities who were forecasting in their fields of expertise and who turned out to be one hundred percent wrong. Perhaps the most striking example is the forecast implicit in the statement made by the British Astronomer Royal in 1956, that "space travel is utter bilge." The Library of Congress has compiled a very extensive list of expert predictions, entitled "Erroneous Predictions and Negative Comments Concerning Exploration, Territorial Expansion, Scientific and Technological Development." As the title implies, this survey includes not only statements about the feasibility of certain technological advances but also statements about the economic value of geographic and scientific exploration. Every one of the predictions in this survey was made by a distinguished authority who should have been well informed in the field in which he made his prediction, and every one of them was proven wrong, the proof often coming not long after the ink was dry on the page of the forecast.

What is the lesson to be drawn from this? That experts are always wrong, and therefore intuitive forecasts are worthless? Not at all. In the first place, there are many examples of the experts' being right. These examples just don't make as exciting reading as errors do. Second, the fact that people still do consult experts in preference to people who know nothing about a subject indicates that an expert is more likely to be right than is a non-expert. Putting it another way, even though an expert may be wrong, his intuitive forecast may still be the best forecast available. This, in fact, is the nub of the problem. The real trouble with intuitive forecasting, according to Lenz, is that it is "impossible to teach, expensive to learn, and excludes any process of review." The real goal is not to get rid of the experts but to devise methods which are teachable and which are less intuitive and more explicit, so that it becomes possible to have a forecast checked by

several people, just as any engineering design or calculation can be
checked.

CONSENSUS METHODS

One of the simplest methods of overcoming some of the disadvantages
of intuitive forecasts is the use of a panel of experts. The notion behind this is that the interaction between several experts is more likely
to ensure consideration of aspects which any single individual might over-
look. More of the factors bearing on a situation are likely to be considered, and there is a better chance that a hidden bias of one panel
member will be offset by a contrary bias in another member. The forecast may be prepared by a panel meeting face to face, or it may be prepared by a panel which never meets but interacts in other ways.

Probably the most common type of consensus forecast is that prepared
by a panel which meets together. This method has proven successful in
the past. The U.S. federal government, especially the Department of Defense, has made extensive use of this method. One of the largest groups
ever assembled for this purpose was the Air Force's Project Forecast,
which had representatives from 30 Department of Defense organizations,
10 non-DOD federal organizations, 26 universities, 70 industrial corporations, and 10 not-for-profit corporations. These people were organized into 12 technology panels and 5 capability panels. They met during
a six-month period in 1963 and produced a 14-volume report on the technology required to meet the defense needs of the 1970s.

Despite the widespread use and apparent success of face-to-face panels, they do have a number of disadvantages, all stemming from the well-
known problems of committee action. A dominant personality may unduly
influence the results. Fatigue of the group as a whole may result in a
false consensus. There may be an unwillingness on the part of members
to abandon a publicly expressed opinion, even after hearing contrary
arguments. And there is the opposite possibility of producing a watered-
down least common denominator out of a desire to avoid offending anyone.

In an attempt to overcome these difficulties, researchers at the
Rand Corporation devised the "Delphi Procedure," which makes use of a
panel of experts to arrive at a consensus but avoids the drawbacks of
committee action by using a series of questionnaires instead of having
the committee members meet face to face. In the first questionnaire,
they are asked to make their forecasts on the topic of interest. The
replies are compiled as a composite forecast, which shows the extent of
the differences of opinion among the members of the panel but preserves
the anonymity of the panelists and their opinions. In the second questionnaire, the panelists are asked to comment on the composite forecast
and give reasons why they disagree with the composite result, if they do
disagree. In the third and subsequent questionnaires, the panelists are
presented with the current composite forecast as well as a summary of
the reasons the panelists gave for changing it (i.e., arguments as to why
an event would take place earlier or later than the majority of the panel
thinks it will).

In each succeeding round of questionnaires, the panelists are expected to consider the arguments of the other panelists and either defend
their positions with counterarguments or change their positions to agree
with the majority. The anonymity of the procedure makes it easier for
the panelists to consider arguments on their merits, without being

influenced by their personal opinions of the panelists who originated the
argument. In addition, panelists find it easier to abandon their earlier
positions without losing face, if they become convinced that their earlier positions were in error. In practice, four or five rounds of questionnaires are sufficient for the panelists to converge on an agreed prediction. Figure 1 shows the behavior of one experimental Delphi panel on

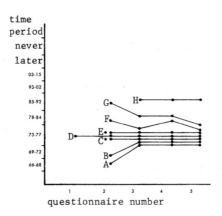

Fig. 1. Converging estimates of the date of an event.

a single question: the estimated date of an anticipated event. The three
panelists in the middle retained their original opinion. The two "early"
and two "late" panelists revised their initial opinions to converge toward
the middle. One member, holding an extreme position, neither influenced
the remainder of the panel nor was influenced by it. The result is typical of panel behavior in a Delphi sequence. Some experiments at Rand indicate that the Delphi Procedure does improve the accuracy of group forecasts, but the method is too new to have received extensive validation.
It does offer considerable promise and undoubtedly will be more widely
used in the future. One of the biggest Delphi panels ever formed was used
by the corporate planning office of TRW, Inc., to obtain a technological
forecast in the areas of technology of most concern to the company.

FORECASTING ANALOGY

        This method attempts to find analogies between the thing to be fore-
cast and some historical event or well-known physical or biological process. To the extent that the analogy is a valid one, the original event
or process can be used to make a prediction about the future development
of some area of technology.

        The use of historical analogy is actually quite common in everyday
life. Expressions such as "We tried something like that once before and
here's what happened" are certainly well known to everyone. The major
difference between the ordinary use of historical analogy and its use in
technological forecasting is that the technological forecaster uses it
consciously and deliberately, examining the "model" situation and the
situation to be forecast in considerable detail to determine the extent
to which the analogy between them is valid. The introduction and spread
of an earlier technological innovation, the social impact of some

previous invention, the delay between the introduction of some specific
technology in one social situation and its introduction in some other
and different situation, the delay between the adoption of a specific
technology in a certain industry and the adoption of a successor technology in the same industry - all are illustrations of historical situations that can be used as models for predicting the future progress of
some technology under study. Even though history never repeats itself
exactly, the use of historical analogies can give considerable insight
into the likely course of development of some technology of current interest. An example of an extensive use of this approach is the book, *The
Railroads and the Space Program: An Exploration in Historical Analogy*
(Bruce Mazlish, ed.). As the title indicates, the contributors to this
volume attempted to find similarities between the U.S. space program and
the development of the railroads in the nineteenth century and to use
these similarities to make predictions about the space program.

Another type of forecast by analogy, much less common in everyday
life but in fairly wide use by technological forecasters, is the analogy with physical or biological processes. An especially common approach
is the use of growth curves to predict the advance of some technology.
Both individuals and populations of many living species have growth curves
that follow an S shape. It has been observed that many technological devices follow this same pattern - a slow start, then a rapid rise, followed
by a leveling off and obsolescence. Figure 2 shows clear-cut examples of

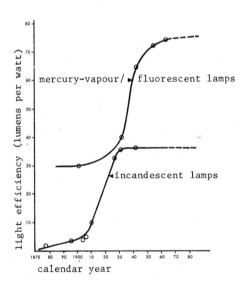

Fig. 2. S-shaped growth curves of lighting devices.

this pattern in the field of illumination technology. Here two specific
classes of devices illustrate this growth pattern. There are actually
good reasons for the similarily between growth in performance of a technological device and the growth of an individual or population. In both,
growth tends to be the cumulative result of a large number of separate
accretions or advances, and there are often considerable difficulties to
be overcome at the outset, causing the growth to be slow. Once these

difficulties are overcome, the stage is set for rapid growth, until some
limit is encoutered. Biologically, this limit is usually environmental,
such as a fixed food supply. Similarly in technology, the limit is
usually "environmental" in the sense that it is extrinsic to the technology-generation process. It frequently comes from some natural limit on
the performance of some specific class of device. Since technologies
do tend to follow the S-shaped growth curve, it appears natural to try
to forecast technological progress by using this method. It is especially applicable to technologies where there is some known upper limit to
the possible performance, such as the speed of light or the achievement
of 100 percent efficiency.

     The major strength of this method is that it eliminates much of
the subjectivity of either intuitive or consensus methods of forecasting.
Its major weakness, however, is that the exact extent of the analogy between the model and the thing to be forecast is often not evident until
too late to do any good. For instance, the plot of performance versus
time for some device often gives no advance warning that the curve is
going to change from slow start to rapid growth or pass through the in-
flection point and slow down. The points at which these changes occurred
can often be recognized only in retrospect. Thus, useful as this method
is, it does not completely satisfy the needs of the technological forecaster. There is still a need for methods which, like the use of analogies, eliminate the subjectivity of expert opinion but which make better
use of past data to develop predictions of when higher level of performance will be reached.

TREND EXTRAPOLATION

     Trend extrapolation is one way of getting around the problem of
predicting when the S-curve is going to change direction. Instead of
concentrating on a single device and attempting to predict the future
course of development of that device, the trend extrapolation method
considers a series of successive devices which performed similar functions. These can be considered individual representatives of a broad
area of technology. It is then necessary to find a single performance
characteristic of these devices that can be exrpessed numerically.
The forecast is made by plotting the performance of each device against
the year in which it was achieved. If a trend is apparent, this trend
is projected and becomes the forecast. An example is shown in Fig. 3,
which considers the same area of technology as Fig. 2, that is, illumination technology. Instead of plotting the course of development of
a single device, however, each successively developed device becomes
a single point on the curve. Note that even though not all the devices
shown in the figure are electrical in nature, the energy consumption of
each of them can be converted into watt-equivalents, so that a uniform
ordinate, efficiency in lumens per watt, can be used for the devices.
While several points could be plotted for each device, there is usually
no value in doing so. Successive devices usually have major differences
in performance, on the order of 100 percent or more, while improvements
to a single device usually are on the order of a few percent. If the
curve were drawn in detail, with several points for each device, and if
an accurate representation were made of the plateaus usually reached by
specific devices, the curve would actually be in stairsteps. The
straight line shown is the envelope of the true curve. Hence this method of forecasting is sometimes referred to as the use of "envelope
curves."

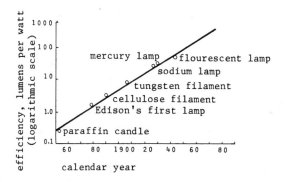

Fig. 3. Trend in improvement of illumination devices.

Use of trend extrapolation in this way avoids the problem of making detailed predictions about the development of specific devices. On the other hand it provides less information about the actual devices that will make it possible to achieve the predicted performance. The curve says only that the performance will be attained. It does not say anything about whether existing devices can be improved to attain that performance or whether a new device will be invented.

There is a useful variant of the straightforward form of trend extrapolation, known as the precursor method. It involves finding a relationship between two areas of technology with one leading the other by a predictable interval. An example is shown in Fig. 4, which compares

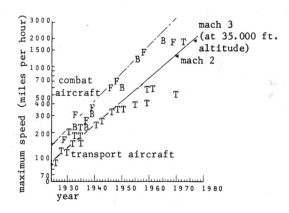

Fig. 4. Spead trends of combat and transport aircraft.

the top speeds of U.S. combat aircraft with those of U.S. transport aircraft. As the trend lines indicate, combat aircraft appear to be leading transport aircraft by a slowly widening gap. On the assumption that these trends will continue, such a graph could be used to predict the future speed of transport aircraft, based on already-achieved speeds of combad aircraft. The credibility of this type of forecast is higher

than that of a straighforward trend extrapolation, especially where
there is some logical connection between the two trends. Such a connection is plausible in the case of combat and transport aircraft.
However, in some apparently correlated trends, there may be no logical
connection whatsoever between the two technologies. Hence the method
must be used with care. In any case, the method cannot be used for
making projections farther ahead than the lag times between the two
technology areas.

To digress a little, the data shown in Fig. 4 can also be considered as two examples of straightforward trend projection. As such,
they contain some interesting features. The highest-speed bomber
point on the graph represents the SR-71, which was developed in secret
by Lockheed for the Air Force. The date shown for it is the date its
existence was publicly announced, and the speed shown is its publicly
announced speed. Since it was probably operational before its existence was announced, the point should probably be moved to the left.
Also its actual top speed probably exceeds that publicly announced and
the point should be moved higher. Applying either or both of these
"correction factors" would move the point closer to the trend line for
combat aircraft. The lesson here is that even secret technological advances tend to follow the same trends as preceding nonsecret advances.

Now consider the points representing transport aircraft. As they
show, there has been essentially no increase in top speeds for new
transports throughout the 1960s. This resulted from the following factors: operation at speeds just below mach 1.0 produces difficulties
associated with the onset of compressibility and formation of shock
waves; operation just above mach 1.0 is highly uneconomic because of
high drag penalties; the technology needed to operate in the efficient
but high-temperature, high-supersonic regime was not yet available in
transport aircraft. As a result, several successive transport designs
continued to have top speeds in the neighborhood of 550 knots. If the
graph showed all the civilian transports introduced in the 1960s, the
impact of these factors would appear even more clearly. However, the
highest transport point shown (actually a prediction, since it has not
been achieved yet) is for the supersonic transport (SST). Once the
technology became available to permit operation at speeds near mach
3.0, where operation is much more efficient than at speeds just above
mach 1.0, transport design reverted to the trend line followed by most
preceding transports. The factors that dominate transport design were
temporarily stymied by the difficulties of transonic operation, but
once this barrier was hurdled they again exerted their control.

Trend extrapolation, whether of the straightforward variety or the
precursor method, is at once the simplest and most sophisticated method of technological forecasting currently available. In concept it
is quite simple. It involves only the plotting of some quantitative
characteristic of the technology against time and extrapolating any
observable trend. But sophistication can enter this process quite
rapidly, one of the first possible sources being the choice of the
characteristic to be plotted. In the case of aircraft, for instance,
speed is a fairly obvious characteristic. However, for transport aircraft, productivity, measured in tons payload × miles-per-hour cruis-
ing speed, is somewhat less obvious but is more directly related to
their real function than is top speed. (Such a plot, incidentally,
would show that throughout the 1960s, the productivity of successive
new models of transport aircraft grew steadily, even though the top
speed remained relatively static.) In any event, considerable

sophistication may be involved in choosing a characteristic that not
only truly represents the ability of devices to function as expected
but also can be applied to successive devices that may operate on different principles while performing the same function. Likewise, choosing the scale on which to plot the characteristic is not always simple.
Probably a logarithmic scale is most frequently used. Others such as
cumulative normal distribution, cumulative log-normal distribution,
etc., may be used. The usual purpose in choosing a scale is to allow
the trend, if any, to show as a straight line. For instance, if the
growth of the characteristic being plotted is expected to be exponen-
tial, plotting on a logarithmic scale will produce a straight line.
If the scale is poorly chosen, the trend may be nonlinear and therefore hard to project. Finally, even with a characteristic and a scale
carefully chosen, the points do not usually lie on a smooth curve.
Drawing a trend line may involve nothing more than an "eyeball" fit
with a straighedge, or it may involve sophisticated mathematical curve-
fitting techniques. Thus while trend extrapolation is simple in principle, it can rapidly become sophisticated in use.

    However, whether the extrapolation method is used in its conceptual
simplicity or involves some sophisticated mathematical techniques, it is
based on an important underlying assumption: that the conditions which
prevailed in the past and were responsible for the well-behaved trend
observed in the data will continue unchanged into the future, at least
as far as the time of the desired prediction. No amount of mathematical
sophistication in treatment of the data can make up for the breakdown,
of this assumption. In many cases, though, the exact nature of the conditions responsible for a trend is not even known, let alone whether
they will remain constant. But suppose it is known that some relevant
conditions are going to change. Then it may no longer be possible to
make a prediction by extrapolating past trends. For instance, suppose
a majority of the public decided it simply would not tolerate the operation of an SST over inhabited land areas. Under these changed conditions, a straightforward projection of the past trend in transport aircraft speed would not be justified. Or suppose the government or a
major corporation makes a policy decision to accelerate the growth of
some technology by deliberately changing some relevant condition, such
as level of resources applies - as, for instance, the federal government
did to rocket technology with the decision to put a man on the moon.
Trend extrapolation gives little or no hope of providing accurate forecasts of the progress of the accelerated technology. Not only that, it
gives no guidance as to which conditions should be altered, to achieve
a desired rate of progress. In short, if a change in the relevant conditions is big enough, whether it is forecast but not under anyone's
control or is deliberately introduced by someone, extrapolating past
trends is of little value as a means of forecasting.

STRUCTURAL MODELS

    The structural model represents an attempt to develop a mathemati-
cal or analytical model of the technology-generation process. As with
mathematical models of any process, the purpose of constructing a model
of the technology-generation process is to single out certain elements
as being relevant to the process, make explicit some of the functional
relationships among these elements, and express these functional relationships in mathematical form. A characteristic feature of such models
is that they tend to be abstractions; certain elements are omitted because they are judged to be irrelevant, and the resulting simplification

in the description of the situation is intended to be helpful in analyzing and understanding it.

Fig. 5 shows an example of a model of the technology-generation

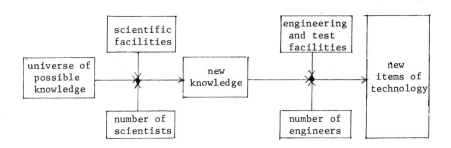

Fig. 5. Structural model of the technology-generation process.

process in block diagram form. This represents an attempt to model the
flow of knowledge, from discovery through engineering into technology.
In principle, a mathematical relationship would specify the rate at
which new knowledge is produced, based on the number of scienctists at
work and the type and extent of scientific research facilities available
to those scientists. Similarly, a mathematical relationship would specify the rate of progress of some parameter of technology (such as lumens per watt, used in Figs. 2 and 3), based on the rate of production
of new knowledge and the engineers and facilities available to exploit
the new knowledge.

Each of the blocks, of course, conceals a submodel. For instance,
the number of scientists available to work in a specific field is not
a static figure. It is increased by migrations from other fields and
by new graduates from colleges. It is decreased by deaths, emigrations,
and diversions of scientists to teaching. Diversion to teaching, while
it may lead to a short-term reduction in the numbers of scientists working full-time in some field, is essential if the number of new graduates
is to be increased. So the number of scientists available over time, is
a result of the interaction of several complex phenomena, some of which
are subject to manipulation as a result of policy choices. Furthermore,
the blocks are not independent of each other. An increase in the amount
of scientific research facilities available can be accomplished by divert-
ing engineers from the exploitation of new knowledge to the design and
construction of new facilities. These submodels and their interactions
are typical of what is involved in constructing a model of the technology-generation process and of finding mathematical expressions for the
relationships among the elements of the model.

What is the current state of the art in constructing structural
models of the technology-generation process? Unfortunately, existing
models are both quantitatively and qualitatively deficient. In the model of Fig. 5, for instance, we simply do not know enough to specify
the mathematical relationship between number of scientists at work in
a field, the amount of research facilities available to them, and the
rate of production of new knowledge. It is clear that the rate of production of new knowledge increases with an increase in the number of

scientists working in a particular field. However, the relationship is
not a simple one, and in particular it is not linear. Simply because
of communication problems, the average rate of discovery per scientist
falls off as the number of scientists in a field increases. Because of
these and many other problems, today it is not possible to make quantitative statements about the relationships shown in the model. At best,
then, such models can only be qualitative.

However, here again the lack of knowledge is a hindrance. The model shown, for instance, implies that technology is produced out of knowledge generated through scientific research. But we know this is not
the full story, either. Many instances of new technology arise out of
sheer empiricism, with science later providing explanation and under-
staning. Thermodynamics, which followed rather than preceded the steam
engine, is only one example. Not enough is known about the empirical
foundations of technology to allow us to construct a model of the technology-generation process that is even qualitatively correct.

Despite the deficiencies of the current models, constructing models
is one of the most promising lines of development in improving our capability to do technological forecasting. First of all, it is clear that
qualitatively and quantitatively correct models of the technology-generation process will allow us to go beyond any of the other currently
used techniques. Second, the research needed to develop the knowledge
to improve current models is fairly well defined and is being actively
pursued at a number of centers. Hence it is fairly safe to predict that
within a few years rudimentary models will be available that will allow
us to make quantitative predictions of the impact on technological
growth of changes in allocation of resources, construction of new facilities, etc. Instead of being forced to assume that conditions will
remain unchanged, we will be able to determine the effect of deliberate
changes in conditions.

Within the past decade or so, technological forecasting has progressed from something resembling a black art to the point where it is
beginning to look like a science. It will probably never approach being
an exact science, since it deals with predicting what human beings will
do, and they are a notoriously unpredictable lot. However, it has already reached the point where we can identify meaningful measures of
technological progress and use them to predict further progress, provided that the conditions which existed in the past remain unchanged.
Under some circumstances, we can even make qualitative predictions
about the impact of policy decisions on technological progress. In
the reasonably near future we can expect to be able to make quantitative predictions about technological progress, given information about
the factors which determine that progress. We should even be able to
make deliberate plans to achieve specified rates of progress and know
what it will cost in men and resources to achieve those rates. When
that day arrives, technological forecasting will be used as regularly
in making business and political decisions as economic forecasting is
now.

The Delphi procedure seems to have attract-
ed a great deal of popular attention. In
fact, even those non-forecasters who know
nothing else about technological forecasting
frequently have at least heard of Delphi.
The previous essay described it briefly, to
put it into context with other methods. However, since so many have heard something
about it, it deserves fuller treatment.
The following essay, by one of the co-inven-
tors of Delphi, Dr. Norman Dalkey of the Rand
Corporation, presents a survey of current
findings about Delphi.

DELPHI

NORMAN C. DALKEY*

The Rand Corporation, Santa Monica, California, U.S.A.

1. INTRODUCTION

Delphi is the name of a set of procedures for eliciting and refining
the opinions of a group of people. In practice, and procedures would be
used with a group of experts or especially knowledgeable individuals.

The significance of the Delphi technique should be examined in the
context of what I call the Advice Community. Both industry and government are served by a large group of consultants who purvey information,
predictions, and analyses to aid the formation of policy and making
decisions. The community is a highly miscellaneous assortment of "in-
house" advisors, and external consultants from academia, other industries, nonprofit corporations, and, of course, any other walk of life
that appears relevant to the problem facing the decisionmaker. Some
of this advice is based on solid generalizations from observation,
either of the "crude" empirical variety or somewhat more prestigious
deductions from established scientific principles. A great deal of it
is "opinion."

The notion of opinion is extremely fuzzy, but with your indulgence,
I would prefer not to try to make it precise. With respect to the interests of this conference, I believe you will agree that in the area
of long range forecasting of technological and social developments there
is an especially large admixture of opinion. For this area, the creation
of techniques for refining opinion is of particular interest.

Pragmatically, a basic characteristic of opinion as opposed to more
solid knowledge is the fact that if you interrogate several equally competent individuals, you are likely to get a divergence of answers. This
is obviously not a defining characteristic, since uniformity of response
does not guarantee the solidity of that response. From the standpoint

*Any views expressed in this paper are those of the author. They
should not be interpreted as reflecting the views of The Rand Corporation
or the official opinion or policy of any of its governmental or private
research sponsors. Papers are reproduced by The Rand Corporation as a
courtesy to members of its staff.

This paper was prepared for presentation to the Second Symposium
on Long-Range Forecasting and Planning, Almagordo, New Mexico, October
11-12, 1967.

of the decisionmaker, a divergence of estimates creates a problem of how
to use the estimates in fashioning his policies. There are several heuristic devices that are traditional in the advice community. One is to
select a single advisor on some grounds (ranging all the way from personal friendship to lustre within the community). This usually guarantees
a certain uniformity. Another is to involve several knowledgeable individuals and employ some method of group interaction to arrive at a
common opinion. The most popular of such methods is that of the committee, or commission, with a variety of informal ways to arrive at the
"sense of the committee."

Selection of a single advisor in "soft" areas is clearly fraught
with danger; on the other hand, committees have certain drawbacks which
have been dramatized by a large number of investigations by psychologists and small-group sociologists over the past two decades [1]. One
major drawback is the influence of the dominant individual. A quite
convincing group of studies have shown that the group opinion is likely
to be highly influenced, if not determined, by the views of the member
of the group who does the most talking, and that there is no significant
correlation between success in influencing the group and competence in
the problem being discussed. Another difficulty which has not received
as much attention in the literature is "noise" - irrelevant or redundant
material that obscures the directly relevant material offered by participants. A third difficulty is group pressure that puts a premium on
compromise.

2. DELPHI PROCEDURES

The Delphi procedures have been designed to reduce the effects of
these undesirable aspects of group interaction. The procedure has three
distinctive characteristics:

1. Anonymity.

2. Controlled feedback.

3. Statistical "group response."

Anonymity is a device to reduce the effect of the socially dominant
individual. It is maintained by eliciting separate and private answers
to prepared questions. Ordinarily, the procedure is carried out by
written questionnaire; on-line computers have been used for some exercises. All other interactions between respondents is through formal
communication channels controlled by experimenters.

Controlled feedback is a device to reduce noise (among other things).
A Delphi exercise will usually consist of several iterations where the
results of the previous iteration are "fed back" to the respondents, normally in summarized form.

As a representative of the group opinion, some form of statistical
index is reported. For cases where the group task is to estimate a numerical quantity, the median of individual estimates has turned out to
be the most useful index tried to date. Thus, there is no particular
attempt to arrive at unanimity among the respondents, and a spread of
opinions on the final round is the normal outcome. This is a further
device to reduce group pressure toward conformity.

A typical exercise is initiated by a questionnaire which requests estimates of a set of numerical quantities, e.g., dates at which technological possibilities will be realized, or probabilities of realization by given dates, levels of performance, and the like. The results of the first round will be summarized, e.g., as the median and inter-quartile range of the responses, and fed back with a request to revise the first estimates where appropriate. On succeeding rounds, those individuals whose answers deviate markedly from the median (e.g., outside the inter-quartile range) are requested to justify their estimates. These justifications are summarized, and fed back, and counter-arguments elicited. The counter-arguments are in turn fed back and additional reappraisals collected. This basic pattern has, of course, many possible variants, only a few of which have been tried.

The procedure has been exercised with material where there is no immediate way to evaluation the results - e.g., long range technological and social developments - and also with material where there is the possibility of checking, such as short range economic predictions and estimates of quantities where the actual figures are obtainable, typically "almanac type" material. For material where confirmation is possible, typical outcomes are that opinions tend to converge during the experiment, and more frequently than not, the median response moves in the direction of the true answer. In the case of material where confirmation is not possible, all we can say is that opinions do converge during the exercise [2], [3].

One additional feature of present Delphi procedures should be mentioned. Respondents are requested to make some form of self-rating with respect to the questions. Several different kinds of self-ratings have been tried - ranking the questions in the order of the respondents judgment as to his competence to answer them; furnishing an absolute estimate of the respondent's confidence in his answer; estimating a relative self-confidence with respect to some reference group. In general there has been no significant correlation discovered between such self-ratings and *individual* performance for confirmable estimates. However, it has usually been possible to use the self-ratings to select a subgroup of relatively more confident individuals where the performance of the subgroup has been slightly, but consistently better than the group as a whole. In one very thorough study, the improvement was obtained only by combining two self-rating indices - ranking of questions, and absolute estimates of confidence [4].

3. RESULTS OF EXPERIMENTS

There are many things we do not understand as yet about the information processing going on during a Delphi exercise. Thus, we cannot as yet determine how much of the convergence is due to three different factors which are clearly at work: (1) social pressure, (2) "rethinking" the problem, (3) transfer of information during feedback. Several exercises have been conducted that throw some light on this. In one [5], a set of twenty almanac type questions were posed to a group of 23 respondents. A control group of 11 respondents were given the same questions, but on the second round were simply asked to reasses their answers, with no feedback whatsoever. They were not even told what their previous responses had been. In general, except for two questions, the amount of convergence was comparable for the two groups, and the accuracy of responses for the control group was as good for the second-round responses of the experimental group. This would appear to indicate that a major

factor in this exercise was "rethinking." However, the effect of social
pressure and/or information transfer is also indicated by the fact that
for the experimental group the interquartile ranges of the second round
responses were uniformly contained in the interquartile ranges of the
initial responses, whereas for the control group the second-round ranges
were contained in the initial ranges for only thirteen out of the twenty
questions.

To try to pin down a little more the factors involved, we conducted
an experiment this summer comparing the performance of structured face-
to-face discussion groups and the anonymous questionnaire technique.
The experiment was guided by two presumptions. (Hypotheses is too pre-
tentious a notion in this rather unstructured subject.) The first presumption was that in a face-to-face situation, information transfer is
likely to be much greater than in the anonymous controlled communication
situation. This would presumably tend toward greater accuracy on the
part of the conference estimates. The second presumption was that the
effect of undesirable social interactions could be meliorated by impos-
ing a specific format for the discussions. The format employed was:
for each question a new discussion leader was selected by chance, the
leader listed on a blackboard all relevant information (including
"opinions") suggested by members of the group; he then listed as many
different approaches (little "models") for answering the question as
the group could devise; estimates were made by each approach; and finally a group consensus was arrived at by informal agreement.

The presumption to be tested was that a structured conference of
this sort would produce more accurate estimates than the questionnaire
technique. The experiment was performed using a group of graduate
students engaged in summer consultant activities at Rand. There were
ten participants, divided into two groups of five. There were twenty
questions, of the almanac sort, divided into four sets of five. Each
participant group answered ten of the questions by questionnaire, and
ten by structured discussion. The only innovation in the Delphi procedure was to interpose a pure information round between the first and
second estimation round. Each respondent was allowed to ask the group
two questions and the group replies were fed back before the second
estimate was made.

The major outcome of the experiment was that the presumption that
the structured discussion would turn in a better performance was not
born out; in fact, the questionnare responses were, if anything, somewhat more accurate than the structured conference responses. The difference was not significant except for one measure, namely the sums of
ranks of standard scores,* in which the questionnaire technique showed
up as better

For the discussion groups, no adequate measure was obtained for
the role of dominant members, noise, and pressure for consensuses; but

---

*Standard scores were computed by dividing the group estimate by
the true answer. The 40 responses were ranked in order of accuracy,
and the sums of these ranks taken for each configuration (group, method,
question set). The analysis of variance for the sums of ranks indicated
a difference between the two methods significant at the .05 level.

it was clear from observation of the discussions that the structure imposed was inadequate to eliminate these effects.

An interesting anomaly appeared in the performance of the questionnaire groups; namely, the responses on the second round were more accurate than the responses on the fourth (and final) round. Whether this
was due to fatigue - for each set of five questions, the entire set of
responses was obtained in one afternoon session - or due to a satura-
tion effect (all of the relevant information elicited by the second
round, and simply "wandering" estimates from then on) cannot be determined from the data.

Perhaps the significance of the experiment can be most sharply
summed up by the following conclusions: if the conference groups had
been requested to open their session with anonymous individual "guesti-
mates" of the answer to each question, the median of these off-the-
cuff guesses would have been more accurate than the group consensus
obtained after a more or less thorough discussion of the subject.

4. DISCUSSION

Delphi procedures are still in an experimental stage with regard
to applications to the advice process. The evidence is mounting that
systematic processing of expert opinion can produce significant improvements both in accuracy and reliability (using the notion of reliability
to refer to the range of estimates). However, the role of Delphi procedures within the corpus of forecasting techniques - extrapolation,
simulation, demand analysis, gaming, etc. - has not been established.
In particular, there are no cases that I know of where Delphi procedures have been explicitly employed to support specific policy decisions. Hence, there are no direct comparisons of the relative effectiveness of the procedures vs. other more traditional forms of advice.
The studies that I am familiar with in areas relevant to policy have
been more like exploratory exercises to test the feasibility and
"manageability" of the procedures with extensive subject matters and
geographically scattered experts. In this respect, the procedures have
turned out to be manageable, but often rather cumbersome.

A common reaction is to imagine Delphi as a method of obtaining
inputs for some kind of formal estimating structure - e.g., inputs
for a simulation model. I must confess that at times I find this an
appealing notion, but it cannot be the full story. Most often, for
those areas where data is lacking, a formal model is lacking as well.
As a matter of fact, the Delphi procedure is one of the most efficient
I know for "uncovering" the implicit models that lie behind opinions
in the "soft" areas. One of the most valuable side-products of a
Delphi exercise concerned with strategic bombing was the skeleton of
a model which was later fleshed out in great detail [2].

There are several tautologies which are directly relevant to the
group estimation process: (a) The total amount of information available to a group is at least as great as that available to any member.
(b) The median response to a numerical estimate is at least as good
as that of one half of the respondents. (c) The amount of *misinformation* available to the group is at least as great as that available
to any member. (This one is usually overlooked in discussions of the
advantages of groups vs. individuals.) (d) The number of approaches

(or informal models) for arriving at an estimate is at least as great for the group as for any member. (c) Corresponding item for approaches is as (c) for information. For simplicity I have included noise in misinformation and poor approaches.

These tautologies do not add up to anything like a "theory" of the group estimation process, but they are suggestive. For example, (c) and (e) hint that there may be an optimal size of group for a given kind of estimation. This would be in accordance with some experimental results with small discussion groups. They also suggest that part of the group estimation process should be concerned with active suppression of misininformation as well as "filling voids" in information.

We have no way at present of determining whether the questionnaire-feedback procedure is anything like an optimal use of the information available to a group, or whether it includes a mechanism for reducing the effect of misinformation. Nor can we say that it is most effectively used in isolation, or within the context of other methodologies. In short, there is a very large field waiting for the plough.*

REFERENCES

1.   MAIER, N.R.J., Assets and Liabilities in Group Problem Solving: The Need for an Integrative Function, *Psychological Review, 74,* 4, pp. 239-249, July 1967.

2.   DALKEY, N., and HELMER, O., An Experimental Application of the Delphi Method to the Use of Experts, *Management Science, 9,* 458-467, 1963.

3.   GORDON, T.J., and HELMER, O., *Report on a Long-Range Forecasting Study,* The Rand Corporation, P-2092, September 1964.

4.   CAMPBELL, R. A Methodological Study of the Utilization of Experts in Buriness Forecasting, *unpublished Ph.D. dissertation,* ICLA, 1966.

5.   BROWN, B., and HELMER, O., *Improving the Reliability of Estimates Obtained from a Consensus of Experts,* The Rand Corporation, P-2986, September 1964.

6.   DALKEY, N. *The Delphi Method: An Experimental Study of Group Opinion,* The Rand Corporation RM-5888-PR, June 1969.

---

*For some additional ploughing see [6].

A charge frequently levelled against
the technological forecaster is,
"you can't predict a breakthrough".
The intended implication is that
since you can't predict a breakthrough, technological forecasting
is useless. In the following essay, Mr. Doyle takes up this challenge and argues that you can in
fact predict a breakthrough.

HOW TO PLOT A BREAKTHROUGH

LAUREN B. DOYLE

Technomics, Inc., 1455 19th St., Santa Monica, California 90404, U.S.A.

ABSTRACT

Will there be a breakthrough in the field of information retrieval?
One authority in that field has said, "No." This paper adopts the opposite viewpoint, and speculates on what the elements of such a breakthrough
might be if it were to occur.

Several breakthroughs in other fields are scrutinized in order to
highlight the factors which characterize and energize sudden expansion
of new technologies. These factors, plus some factors specific to the
field of information retrieval, are then extrapolated into a "plot for
a breakthrough."

* * *

"Breakthrough" is a word with military-journalistic origins which
was apparently first used, in a large-scale way, to pertain to the breach
of the German lines in Normandy during the summer of 1944, and the subsequent race by Patton and other elements of the Allied armies to Paris
and points east. Since the war, the word has been repeatedly used to
refer to a phonomenon which has become especially frequent in the last
two decades - the "technological breakthrough." In analogy to the military breakthrough, there is the entrenched enemy of a formidable technical problem, the breach made by some powerful new approach or technique,
and the exploitation spearheads, which may fan out in many unexpected
directions.

As is usually the case with glamour-infused terms, vulgarization
sets in, so that anybody and everybody can benefit from the "psychological fall-out" of the usage of the term. When so many people use a
word like "breakthrough" in connection with promotional efforts, the
use of the word soon becomes suspect, and those few who still employ
the word in an honest way are often themselves forced to find still
another word to describe what they are talking about.

Nevertheless, the word "breakthrough" is just as much here to
stay as is the phenomenon to which it refers. Furthermore, if we
understand what a breakthrough is, and why and how it takes place, we
are in a much better position to use the word meaningfully and to shape
research and development efforts in ways to increase the speed of

incipient breakthroughs as they are recognized. One can go even a step
further and assert that, knowing all the major characteristics and possibilities of a given problem area, one can actually plot a breakthrough.
It is admittedly a tricky thing to do - and failure is overwhelmingly
probable - but success is possible.

What are the defining attributes of a breakthrough? As we enumerate
them here, in each case we are going to look at some pattern of events
in history which displays the enumerated attribute along with other typical breakthrough attributes.

The first attribute is the *relative shortness of time** over which a
breakthrough materializes and grows to maturity. This can be illustrat-
ed by what was perhaps the first genuine breakthrough in the history of
man - the control of fire. Man is said to be a tool-making animal, but
his development in the use of tools proceeded with painful slowness over
tens of thousands of years; the use of tools by humans could be called
a breakthrough only in the perspective of geological time.

The exploitation of fire, however, appears to have been a more ex-
plosive development than anything which had happened previously in the
history of man, occurring within a two-or-three-thousand-year period at
the end of the last Ice Age. Great herds of animals - bison, deer, mas-
todons - were set upon by torch-bearing bipeds who ignited the countryside for miles around. Driven by walls of flame into cul-de-sacs such
as gullies or waterholes, animals not already roasted were picked off
individually by other bipeds wielding spears.

As man surged forward in the wake of the retreating glaciers, he
brought fire with him as a new technology, adaptable to a great variety
of purposes. Its use in trapping and cooking the flesh of animals
changed man from an omnivore to a highly successful carnivore. Its
nocturnal warmth increased man's survivability in cold climates, and
its light held the wolves at bay. The remaining ashes became the first
effective fertilizer, paving the way to the beginnings of agriculture.
Several millenia would yet pass before the first agricultural civilizations, and the bronze and iron technologies made possible by the fire,
but in those first newly-placed centuries of reckless exploitation,
Prometheus did indeed confer his gift.

A second attribute is a *latent need* which, expressed or unexpressed,
provides the climate of receptivity in which new methods are sought,
recognized, and accepted when found. The rise of the "gaslight era"
shows us that the stage was being set for a breakthrough as enormous in
scope as the Industrial Revolution itself - the electrification of civilization. The portals through which the breach was effected were the
electric light and the alternating-current system. As time goes on,
breakthroughs reach maturity faster; if man's first breakthrough took
several thousand years, his "electrifying breakthrough" took less than
40 years.

A large part of our tradition of "invention" seems centered among
those who provided the instruments by which the age of electricity
could be realized: Edison, Bell, Marconi, Tesla, and Lee de Forest.
There were dozens of lesser names who nonetheless made contributions
which in a less spectacular age would have brought them status as first-
rank inventors. For example, in 1879 - the same year in which Edison

---

*This attribute is descriptive, whereas those to follow are con-
tributory or causative.

devised the first successful electric lamp - von Siemens exhibited in
Berlin the first electric street car which used an external power
source rather than a battery.

How many near-inventors and almost-inventors there were during those
times we can't know, but we do know that the countryside abounded - in
the 1860's - with mechanically oriented people who felt strongly that
electricity, the mysterious, invisible, and inconceivable force-fluid
which somehow found its way through solid wires, to make strange things
happen at distant points, was a genie which could be mastered to do man's
bidding.

Moreover, electricity was "clean," whereas coal smoke and gas fumes
were dirty; it was much easier to string wire than to fit pipes together,
and easier to flick a switch than to turn a valve and light a match. The
need for electricity was latent - but perceived and understood by a large
enough number that the breakthrough was practically obliged to happen.

This latent need constitutes only half of the driving force behind
a breakthrough; the other half comes from the emergence of *clearly superior new methods*, the third attribute of a breakthrough. Arguable superiority is not enough; superiority must be incontrovertible. In the con-
test to which we have just alluded, electric light versus gas light, the
problems of constructing untried and unfamiliar electric power distribution networks were so great that such enterprises might not have been
attempted except for the fact that, once the electric light had been
shown feasible, almost anyone could see that the use of electricity was
superior in almost every important respect to the use of gas, even when
a battery was the electric power source.

In modern times one of the best illustrations of this principle is
found in the transistor. In the ever-shorter time spans in which breakthroughs are taking place, we find less than a decade has elapsed between
the first public announcement of the transistor's invention and the large-
scale manufacture of transistorized computers and other devices, and today, after only fifteen years, transistors are the basis of a billion-
dollar industry.

In part this rapid progress was energized by the requirement for
miniaturization and low power in airborne and satellite computers. But
the transistor, quite apart from the special needs of modern weapons
systems, has such general superiority over vacuum tubes that a breakthrough could have been expected in any event, once the characteristics of the transistor were made known to the technological community.

The vacuum tube is fragile, cumbersome, and wasteful of power, its
fragileness leads to unreliability and to sensitivity to shock and vi-
bration; its cumbersomeness requires complex instruments such as computers to be bulky and spread out over entire floors, like the stacks in
a public library; its high consumption of power leads not only to unneces-
sary operating expense, but also creates added engineering problems con-
nected with heat removal, especially when much electronic equipment is
required to be in a confined space, as in an aircraft or aboard ship.
But the transistor has none of these disadvantages.

The transistor, then, is one of the more remarkable examples of
across-the-board superiority of a new technique over an old one that
makes a breakthrough "in the cards." How many other examples are found,
in history, of rapid technological expansion following widespread realization of superiority of method? It would be difficult to cite them

all. There are irrigation (3000 B.C.), movable type (1450 A.D.), steam
power (1770), railroads (1804), telephony (1876), radioactive tracers
(1934), aplification by stimulated emission (masers, lasers, 1951).
These are only a few of the more spectactular examples.

A fourth attribute of a breakthrough is adequacy of available supporting technology. Perhaps there was a need for automatic computation
machinery in 1823; perhaps Babbage's method of mechanical computation
was clearly superior to anything in sight; unfortunately, the supporting
technology required for the feasibility of Babbage's system did not yet
exist.

There are other less dramatic examples of situations where the need
and the superior method were both available, but where the actual breakthrough was postponed until the required supporting technology was developed. Though Lee de Forest invented the three-element vacuum tube which
made radio reception feasible in 1906, radio broadcasting did not come
to pass until 1921; manufacturing methods were just not good enough prior
to that time to assure reasonable reliability of performance in an electronic device even as simple as a radio.

The importance of "adequacy of available supporting technology" is
not to be underestimated merely because it is given here as the fourth
attribute, rather than as one of the first three. There have been times
when either the reality of the need or the superiority of method was not
yet clear enough to be seen by those who needed most to see it, but where
supporting technology together with a handful of imaginative entrepre-
neurs turned the tide toward breakthrough.

When intercontinental rocketry began in the early 1950's, the accent
both in the U.S. and Russia was on liquid-fueled systems; solid-fueled
rockets were thought of as nothing more than glorified artillery shells.
The U.S.,however, had the good fortune to have a highly developed organic polymer technology, which included synthetic rubber and plastics.
Some of the organic polymer industries saw that there was a future for
them in solid propellants and began, more or less on their own, to plot
what would eventually become a breakthrough.

The major problem was to influence the people who held the purse-
strings in the Defense Department to finance the more expensive phases
of development of large-solid-fueled boosters, and it was at this point
that the "clear superiority of method" slowly began to assert itself.
Even here progress was difficult, because those factions with vested
interests in liquid-propellant system development were most persuasive
in their arguments to the effect that solid fuels were inherently
inferior. One problem was the seemingly inadequate thrust of solid
fuels. Another was the problem of cutoff control; stopping a solid-
fueled rocket with the proper velocity was achieved seemed about as
difficult as stopping an erupting volcano.

As we now know, problems of the above sort were not insoluble, but
required only a reasonably steadfast application of engineering know-
how and ingenuity. In Russia, with its somewhat underdeveloped petro-
chemical industry and its trailing position in the development of compact nuclear warheads, the case for solid-fueled intercontinental missiles was never strong enough - during the 1950's - to justify the
developmental investment.

Doubtlessly most of us remember the first newsreel shorts of a Polaris missile being fired from its submerged mobile launching paid. What we saw was slightly incredible: a ridiculous "pop bottle" thrusting itself out of the ocean, drunkenly igniting itself, and taking off like a Fourth of July rocket - in great contrast to the agonizing slowness of the initial flight of an Atlas or a Titan. No one could then deny that a breakthrough had achieved maturity.

As preparation for discussion "How to Plot a Breakthrough," we review the attributes so far discussed, with an indication that each must be taken into account if the plot is to succeed.

1. RELATIVE SHORTNESS OF TIME

This attribute was presented first because it describes what our goal is: to bring to a state of widespread application a new technology whose principles are understood at the outset by perhaps no more than half a dozen people, in a period of time which is quite short in comparison with typical technological gestation periods. Commercial atomic power is an example of a non-breakthrough in the sense that, though the principles of technology were understood in 1942, essentially twenty years were required to achieve the state of "widespread application." In today's times a self-respective breakthrough should take no longer than five years.

2. LATENT NEED

This factor were presented second because, though it is a driving force for a breakthrough, it is a most difficult force to harness. If one attempts to "plot a breakthrough" and fails, it is very likely because he does not understand how to assess and capitalize on the need factor. A technical person may have the educational qualifications and experience to see where there is a breakthrough to be made - and even be right - but be fatally unaware of the quasi-political processes by which strategically placed people become convinced that the need does exist and can be met through a new technology. Unless more than a few are induced to develop and apply the new technology, the support required in the early phases of breakthrough cannot be mustered. This decade sees so many "competing breakthroughs" and so many high-pressure types telling consumers - big and small - what they need, that a breakthrough without an adequate public relations apparatus is headed for stagnation before it starts.

3. CLEARLY SUPERIOR METHODS

We think of a man as fortunate indeed if he stumbles onto a method or technique which looms head-and-shoulders in effectiveness over prevailing arts. But it is not necessarily a case of luck; such techniques can be deliberately sought and found (this is why we finance what is known as "research"). The reason so few are rewarded in the search is not so much that most people are unlucky, but that most people do not persist long enough in the search - they are content to invest their time and energy in the first marginally superior idea they encounter. To put it another way, if one aims for Mars and in the process reaches the moon, he becomes satisfied with the lesser goal because he never dreamed that he would be one of the privileged few to stand on the moon.

The avenue, then, to finding clearly superior methods is: don't be satisfied with the moon.

4.   ADEQUACY OF AVAILABLE SUPPORTING TECHNOLOGY

For the technically oriented person this is perhaps the easiest
factor to reckon with in the plotting of a breakthrough. But, of
course, its importance is not to be forgotten for a moment. Indeed
one might begin his breakthrough plot by searching for brand-new supporting technologies which have not been around long enough to have
realized their most important ramifications. Most of the people who
are aware of the power of such a technology are often themselves leanly
supplied with ideas for its exploitation; typical behavior is to apply
the technology on a hit-or-miss basis hoping something good will happen.
As is frequently the case, such technologies are often so potent that
even a random, unthinking attempt at application can sometimes result
in success. If this is so, the prognosis for a carefully planned applications foray is good indeed, assuming of course that the plan is flexible enough to take advantage of unforeseen developments.

The question of "How to Plot a Breakthrough" cannot be answered
in the text of this paper. It is much easier to write about plotting
a breakthrough than it is to plot one and have it thereupon take place.
In one sense it is about as foolish as writing about "How to Make a
Million Dollars" without having first made it. Indeed, even one who
actually makes a million dollars is not necessarily able to give the
public the straight goods on how to make a million. If such a mil-
lionaire were in full possession of the truth about human nature, and
were honest in revealing his knowledge, he might say: "Don't even try
to make a million. There are only a few people who can do it, starting
from scratch, and I'm one of them."

Therefore, even if I had already successfully plotted a breakthrough
I would not be by that token in a position to advise others on the matter. On the other hand, the theme has been emphasized herein that if
breakthrough plotting is at all possible, it can only be accomplished
by studying former breakthroughs and understanding the forces behind them.
If one then looks for equivalent forces in a current problem area, he
stands a good chance of finding them.

Spotting these forces, of course, does not automatically lead to a
successful forecast. On can leave an unrecognized important element
out of his calculations - an element which can lead history in a completely different direction than one might predict. Maybe there is some
unrecognized virtue - for example - in *not* keeping up with literature.
I have found that many professional people are intimidated in their
productivity by their over-awareness of how much the rest of the world
knows. Will more effective contact with the literature only intimidate
them more? Do they intuitively know this, and do they therefore try to
avoid the literature? This paper has tried to include the probable psychological characteristics of the information user in its analysis, but
it may not have gone nearly far enough.

Whatever the case, it is a safe statement that practitioners of
research and development in the field of information retrieval have
steadfastly neglected to appreciate that the mind and psychology of the
information user form the central element in the whole retrieval picture.

Some grudging acknowledgements of this have been made, leading to library use studies and retrieval system evaluation projects. These studies, of course, shed very little light on what people will do when given radically new tools, such as when modern technology is made available. If I may be so bold as to say it, perhaps our studies of the user are not sufficiently "fundamental." One is hard put these days to win support for such research, because it is "too abstract" and "uninteresting." It is "too remote from practical application." And for some strange reason the horizon of "practical application" continues to be bleak. The fundamentals" of human nature, however, will catch up with us whether we know them or not.

This could be a large part of the story of why breakthroughs happen. Do they happen suddenly because they are long overdue? The principle of lasers was described by F.G. Houtermans, a physicist, 30 years ago. Why was there not a gradual development, rather than a sudden breakthrough? Solid-fueled rockets are as old as gunpowder. Why didn't the Germans (who once led the world in the technology of organic chemistry) develop Polaris-like missiles? Electricity and its properties are known about in the times of Napoleon. Why did it take a century to reach the "age of electricity"?

The balloon of dogma and mental rigidity is inexorably expanded by the pressure of events. The tension increases. Then along comes one guy with a pin. The result: poof! Another breakthrough has occurred.

In the preceding essays, it has been argued
that the advance of technology is forecast-
able. In the following essay Mr. Prehoda
suggests a reason for forecasting; namely
that we can accelerate the progress of those
technologies which are desirable. Rather
than wait for the technology to work itself
out, we can set ourselves the deliberate goal
of achieving the forecast level at an earlier
date. Although Mr. Prehoda presents his
arguments in terms of the space program, they
are valid for any socially or economically
desirable program.*

TECHNOLOGICAL FORECASTING AND SPACE EXPLORATION

ROBERT W. PREHODA

Hollywood, Cal., U.S.A.

From the earliest written records we see that man has always attempted to predict the future. The position of prophets, seers and
oracles was always important in ancient societies, for people usually remembered correct forecasts and forgot the times when their "second sight"
was a bit cloudy. The twentieth century has witnessed a steady series of
serious predictions of changes that will shape the coming years and they
have been characterized by increasing accuracy. The reason for this is
that the last few decades have given us a more complete understanding of
the basic laws of the universe, and scientific discovery is usually followed by accurate measurement and then the gradual control of new forces.
In those branches of technology already well supported financially, accurate prediction is becoming increasingly easy and a comparison of various published projections reveals an impressive unanimity. The entire
field of literature that we call Science Fiction has its roots in our
growing ability to understand the broad features of tomorrow.

The preeminent discovery of the twentieth century is the power or
organized applied research and technological development backed up by well
supported basic research with a minimum of constraints on the investi-
gators. This fact is now fully accepted, and the federal government is
investing $15 billion in R & D during the current fiscal year. The ex-
plosive growth of our national investment in science and technology has
created a requirement for more accurate methods of forecasting the probable results of these increasing R & D expenditures. The need for better
long range scientific planning is causing technological forecasting
methodology to be refined into a systematic and increasingly accurate
discipline.

Technological forecasting is a new field of intellectual activity
that will be of vital importance to those of us who are engaged in various phases of space exploration. First I would like to outline the
present status of technological forecasting and then explain how it can
be employed to the benefit of astronauts. Also in this article, technological forecasting will be shortened to T/F. I personally dislike ab-
breviations and hope that T/F will be acceptable to the readers.

T/F may be defined as "the description or prediction of a foreseeable
invention, specific scientific refinement, or likely scientific discovery
that promises to serve some useful function." These are functions that
meet the requirements of industry, the military services, other governmental agencies and the general needs of society.

*Reprinted from: Q.E.D., October, 1966.

39

The prediction of inventions, biomedical advances, and new scientific discoveries does not require that they be described in great detail with precise performance parameters and production cost data. In many cases, T/F can show us that a certain innovation or discovery is very likely to occur within a certain future time period (range in years 19XX to 19XX). The effect that these foreseeable advancements will have on economic, military and social organizations can be described in considerable detail.

T/F is being refined into a precise planning tool for governmental and industrial decision makers. It attempts to forecast useful control over physical and biological phenomena beyond ten years, in some cases up to fifty years in the future. T/F does not attempt to say that a specific technical feat will take place a certain number of years hence. It extrapolates from historic technology development patterns and makes use of our entire pool of scientific knowledge. This data is used to determine what capabilities will be available and when to expect the capabilities, not when to expect their realization. T/F does *not* always forecast the way a capability will be achieved. In some cases it outlines alternate foreseeable means of achieving a capability and points out the most likely technological option. T/F cannot forecast whether or not various technical capabilities will be exercised. While something may become technically feasible it may not be developed because of various restraints (social, political or economic) that may prevent it from being exploited.

T/F attempts to consider some of the *consequences* to industry, government, and society if a technological capability is indeed exercised. In this regard it can be integrated with other forecasting and long-range planning activities involved in economics, politics and international relations. Any consideration of the future must include T/F because our modern western culture is so deeply involved with technology and is already a product of past collective technological advances. By integrating T/F in planning and speculation about the future, we have the opportunity to consider in advance some of the future's technological options prior to the time when they can be realized. The problems and consequences of these future scientific and technological advances can also be considered in advance.

T/F will evolve into a refined interdisciplinarian procedure that will use the scientific method to study the future and promote progress by accelerating technical developments which can offset potential problems. Its foundation is the thesis that our better understanding and control of the laws of nature have given man a new perception, a capacity to predict accurately scientific goals that can be achieved with predetermined effort. T/F is not a political or social discipline. It is largely a new synthesis of economics, science and technology. T/F will eventually cause a basic change in our outlook rather than a new system of production, distribution or methods of altering credit and monetary values. The basic differences between capitalism and communism lie in the areas of production, distribution and ownership. The role of science and its utilization lies outside the limitations of both systems. Consequently T/F methodology can be effectively employed by a capitalistic or communistic society, or by a totalitarian or democratic state.

T/F is fundamentally based on an understanding of the current limitations of science which have been accurately defined by Sir George Thomson:

> Technology is governed by scientific principles, some of which are
> understood, and there is accordingly a basis for prediction ...

developments which do not contradict known principles and which have an obvious utility will in fact be made, probably in the next hundred years. No doubt there will be discoveries which will transcend what now appear major impossibilities, but these are unpredictable, and so are the practical developments which will follow them.

Responsible forecasts can only be made of developments that already exist at some stage in their scientific evolution, either in theory, basic research experiments or prototype devices that are not yet economically practical. In addition to Sir George Thomson's principal requirement, several key ingredients are part of the complete T/F process.

1. It must be recognized that some reasonably well defined technological barrier has brought progress in a field of science (biological or physical) to the point of diminishing return - the top of the "S" shaped curve characteristic of all technological development (see Fig. 2).

2. This "technical barrier" must have a relationship to a recognized urgent need, perhaps not understood by the general public.

3. There must be some advantage in bypassing the subject "technical barrier." This could be a military or non-weapons oriented requirement.

4. There must be at least some conceptual approaches which do *not* violate well-defined natural laws. These can involve techniques of one or more orders of magnitude beyond current technology, including very radical departures from historic approaches to the basic barrier.

5. The ancillary supporting technology, instrumentation, measurement techniques, etc., must be available or capable of being developed to laboratory operational status within a reasonable time period.

6. There must be agreement among responsible members of the scientific community that the conceptual approaches fall within these broad guidelines, and these technical reviewers must have the courage to make favorable recommendations when the respective segments of the "technological forecasting jigsaw puzzle" fall into place.

7. Government officials who influence and control R & D funding must be capable of recognizing the significance of technological advances made possible by Hahn-Strassmann point breakthroughs, and be willing to "fight" for adequately supported programs.

T/F does not produce a passive series of academic forecasts predicting probable future technological changes and their effects. T/F is not a projection of scientific achievements anticipated by a selected date in the future, but a detailed analysis outlining what science can achieve with a specific allotment of resources (scientists, technicians, money and R & D facilities). T/F will become part of the inventive process itself. In a very real way, every inventor starts with a technological forecast - sometimes small - sometimes a very extensive projection.

To forecast coming events accurately, one must first analyze the three stages in the evolution of scientific development. It starts when something becomes theoretically possible, a discovery stage that is brought about by new interpretations of established physical laws. The possibility stage turns to probability when active laboratory work advances with new tools and techniques. The final stage is a proven fact, when the development can be measured and controlled in the laboratory. This is followed by engineering development of various prototype devices based on the new understanding and control of natural phenomena.

The T/F discovery stage is frequently called *The Hahn-Strassmann Point*. This term was first used by the late Dandrige M. Cole, and had its origin in the December 1938 experiments conducted by Otto Hahn and Fritz Strassmann which resulted in the discovery of uranium fission. Lise Meitner had been an earlier member of the team. The publication of these research results permitted an accurate forecast of contemporary nuclear technology which would not have been possible prior to the announcement of this scientific breakthrough. It is extremely important to recognize the fact that the Hahn-Strassmann point has been reached in a field of science and technology development. This is comparatively easy when it is the result of a dynamic research breakthrough such as the discovery of uranium fission. Recognition is much more difficult when it is a synergistic result of interrelated step-by-step progress of a more evolutionary nature. The Hahn-Strassmann point is equally important when it is the result of a number of small, but collectively important scientific advances.

It is becoming increasingly important to recognize the exact moment when possibility in science becomes probability and to forecast accurately technological developments, economic changes and social problems that are likely to result from the practical exploitation of any probable scientific advancement. The full impact of every new technology should be understood in advance to avoid transitional crises. Forecasts of the future based on T/F methodology will give us advance warning of problems that will be the inevitable result of various technical and biological discoveries.

There are a number of foreseeable advances which promise a great impact on space technology. Some of these will be *single* Hahn-Strassmann points such as U_{235} Fission. There will be *collective* advances such as many individual refinements in propulsion, propellents, structures, staging and guidance which permitted the first orbital systems in 1957 and 1958. Other Hahn-Strassmann points will be synergistic like the development of practical thermonuclear weapons in the early 1950's.

T/F methodology is in its infancy but several promising techniques are emerging. Singularly or collectively they promise to permit better prediction of innovation and scientific advancements. In time they may all be combined in systematic, fully integrated forecasts.

TREND CURVES

It has been frequently observed that "five year forecasts are usually optimistic, ten year forecasts are usually conservative, and ten-to-twenty-year-and-beyond forecasts are almost always extremely conservative." Five to ten year forecasts are primarily oriented towards foreseeable technology which has already reached the Hahn-Strassmann point, developments which probably can be achieved with recognition, funding priority and clever refinement within the next twenty years.

"Trend curves" provide a useful tool in making T/F long-range projections beyond twenty years. It appears that the trend curve was independently conceived in the minds of several serious students of the future. Robert A. Heinlein may have been the first technological forecaster to use trend curves in making serious scientific projections. In a recent review of his mid-century forecast, Heinlein wrote: "Extrapolation means much the same as it does in mathematics: exploring a trend.

It means extending its present direction and continuing the shape it has displayed in its past performance, i.e., if it is a sine curve in the past, you extrapolate it as a sine curve in the future, not as a hyperbola, and most certainly not as a tangent straight line."

G. Harry Stine has pointed out that trend curves were first used in accurately forecasting space achievements by the Air Force Office of Scientific Research. The speed trend curve in Fig. 1 shows that each time a new means of transportation was invented, the speed curve for that device rose sharply and finally leveled off, as the practical limit for that device was reached. Each new increase in speed was produced by a

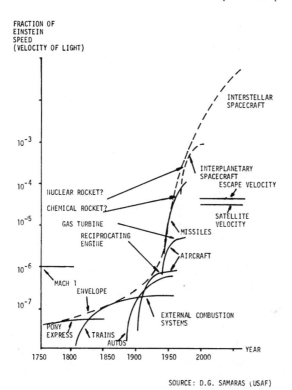

SOURCE: D.G. SAMARAS (USAF)

Fig. 1. Speed trend curve

new device based on a new concept, following a Hahn-Strassmann point discovery or breakthrough. Integrating all the separate technology performance patterns usually produces a trend curve of increasing upward slope.

In 1953, Air Force officials used the speed-trend curve to predict that space exploration was very near, that orbital velocity would be achieved in 1957, and that escape velocity would be achieved by 1959 - right on both. Trend curves can also be misleading. For example:

1. The speed-trend curve indicates that manned spacecraft will achieve speed-of-light accelerations by 1998.

2. The amount of useful controlled energy on the earth will exceed that released by the sun in 1994.

3. The life-expectancy-at-birth curve promises immortality, barring accidents, for anyone born after 2,000 A.D.

4. The population-growth-trend curve suggests that by 3,900 A.D., an expanding solid mass of humanity will be enlarging in all directions at the speed of light.

Since these events are not likely to occur, it is clear that in every field the overall curve must eventually level off or follow an "S" shaped curve. Most developments that experience dynamic growth tend to follow a predictable pattern often referred to as the characteristic "S" shaped curve, sometimes called the "Gompertz curve" after the mathematician who first discovered this statistical phenomenon. (See Fig. 2.).

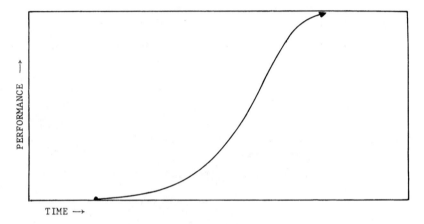

Fig. 2. Gompertz "S" shaped curve

Trend curve prediction must take into account the fact that the extension of a well-established rate of progress will eventually intercept a known physical limit. Since progress by definition cannot extend beyond this limit, only two predictive possibilities exist. The first obviously is that progress will indeed stop at this point. The second is the development of a new technology that will permit the extension of progress beyond previously known limits.

TELESCOPED PERFORMANCE ACHIEVEMENTS

It is in the individual developmental time-achievement trends of each specific technology within an overall area pattern such as transport speed (dependent on propulsion, energy conversion, strength of materials, etc.) that T/F can play a crucial role in years to come. There are actually two different "S" shaped trend curves in each of these technological and biological-control achievement patterns. The schematic in Fig. 3 illustrates this concept. Trend curve A is the pattern of performance achievement that is possible after a Hahn-Strassman point using technological forecasting combined with official recognition and the optimum allocation of resources, funds and qualified specialists. Trend B is the likely achievement pattern if decision makers do not rely on Technological Forecasting and an evolutionary pattern is followed. The full implementation of Technological Forecasting enables us to "telescope performance

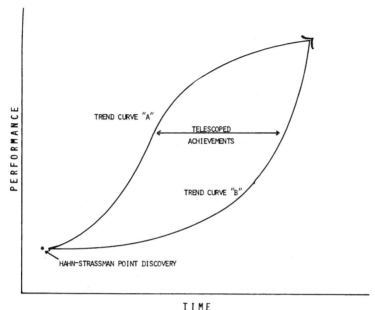

Fig. 3. Telescoped performance gains achieved by full T/F
implementation

achievements", making advanced technology available in a much shorter
period of time. This process can provide decisive terrestrial and space
military systems, increased economic growth and contribute immeasurably
to human happiness.

The most important historic example of the full implementation of
technological forecasting was the American nuclear-weapon demonstrations
in 1945 (Hahn-Strassmann point in 1938). Partial telescoped performance
achievements can be seen in the German V-2 launch in 1942 and the Soviet
orbital satellite launch in 1957 (Hahn-Strassmann points - Konstantine
E. Tsiolkovski's theoretical refinement in 1898, Robert H. Goddard's
performance demonstration in 1926). Full implementation of technological
forecasting in rocketry would have enabled the first satellite to be
launched by 1945, resulting in a time-telescoped performance achievement
of 12 years.

In Fig. 3, trend curve A represents the rate of progress made by the
Manhattan Project scientists in the development of nuclear weapons during
the war. Trend curve B represents the surprisingly slow rate of progress
made by competing German scientists. In contrast, curve A can represent
German rocketry achievements and trend B our unimaginative war-
time rocket development. The V-2 was successfully flown in 1942 and we
did not have a comparable system until the Redstone was launched in 1952.
Full implementation of German rocketry T/F permitted a telescoped-perfor-
mance gain of ten years.

Individual technologies overlap in time and specific purpose. Tele-
scoped-performance achievements can be achieved in every area once the
Hahn-Strassman point is reached. Fig. 4 may illustrate this important

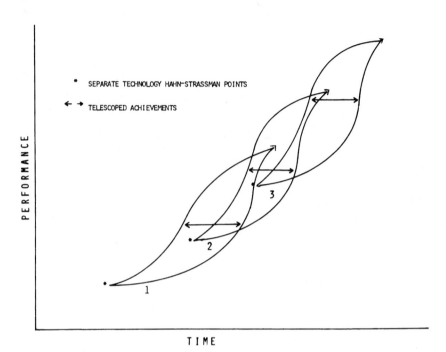

Fig. 4.   Overlapping telescoped performance gains achieved by full
T/F implementation

fact.   Technology envelope 1 may represent foreseeable performance of
chemical rocket propulsion; envelope 2 can represent the possible performance of nuclear rockets.   In the 1970's, the two will be joined in
launch vehicles composed of chemical lower stages and nuclear upper stages.
Technology envelope 3 may represent nuclear-electric or the possibility
of a controlled thermonuclear-propulsion system.   T/F refinement suggests
that we may have nuclear powered earth-to-orbit stages to place a fusion-
propelled spacecraft into orbit where it can economically reach any body
in the solar system.

MATHEMATICAL FORECASTING METHODOLOGY

    Mathematical forecasting methodology makes use of a model which per-
mits complex computer-programmed T/F exercises.   M.I.T.'s J.W. Forrester
has developed Dynamic Forecasting which breaks into numerical inputs the
elements which produce technical progress.   Described in terms of a
dynamic system which includes information feedback control, the principal
components of dynamic forecasting are: (1) engineers and scientists in
training, (2) resulting manpower divided among research, teaching and
other technical occupations, (3) available research facilities, and (4)
output of knowledge and progress.

    Other T/F mathematical approaches are being refined.   Like trend
curves this T/F approach has its advantages and limitations.   It will undoubtedly prove to be a very useful tool when used in connection with
other methods and assist in confirming the probability of foreseeable
rates of progress.

THE DELPHI T/F METHOD

The Delphi T/F method was developed by Dr. Olaf Helmer and Theodore J. Gordon. It avoids the traditional approach toward achieving a consensus through open discussions. The Delphi technique eliminates committee activity altogether, thus reducing the influence of certain psychological factors such as the overriding persuasion of strong personalities, the unwillingness to abandon publicly expressed opinions, and the bandwagon effect of majority opinion. Direct debate is replaced by a carefully designed program of sequential individual interrogations (conducted by questionnaires) interspersed with information and opinion feedback derived by computer consensus from the earlier parts of the program. Some of the questions directed to the respondents may inquire into the reasons for previously expressed opinions, and a collection of such reasons may then be presented to each respondent in the group, together with an invitation to reconsider and possibly revise earlier estimates. Both the inquiry into the reasons and subsequent feedback of the reasons adduced by others may serve to stimulate the experts into taking into due account considerations that had not occurred to them and to give due weight to factors they were initially inclined to dismiss as unimportant.

After the returned questionnaires are analyzed, questions and definitions are reworded or changed in light of the emerging consensus. By repeating the process of sending out increasingly refined questionnaires, the Delphi method permits the individual experts to arrive at a reasonably narrow consensus.

Synthesis Forecasting

No responsible technological forecaster claims that he has the magic formula which will insure success and that all other approaches be discarded. It is generally agreed that as the field progresses, the different approaches will prove to be complementary. As additional time, funding and resources are allotted to technological forecasting, the synthesis or combination of the various methodologies will permit increasingly accurate forecasts to be made.

When one reviews technological forecasts ranging from H.G. Wells' nonfiction *Anticipations* published in 1900 through the years till the present day, one approach has always been used: The intelligence of the individual forecaster. Since many of these men have been distinguished scientists, including several Nobel Laureates, one might call this approach "genius forecasting". There is considerable merit in a forecast made by an open-minded specialist with broad knowledge of other fields that may or may not be related to his discipline. Many extremely intelligent people tend to be "generalists" or persons of "interdisciplinarian" knowledge and interests. They can make singularly good forecasts. They can be brought together in a modified-Delphi approach, and in small working groups "combined genius" forecasts can be refined. Trend curves can be discussed at these meetings. Summary forecasts can be reviewed and brought into proper focus or relationship to a systematic forecast that can include other effective methodological approaches.

Synthesis T/F can start with a preliminary forecast which may be arrived at using trend curves, dynamic forecasting, interviews and correspondence with experts (this can follow the Delphi technique). Information can be from older forecasts. This combination of methodologies can then be synthesized by the T/F refinement teams. There is a lower "critical mass" to the size of these T/F groups. This appears to consist

of one team moderator (the forecaster) and four specialists in one or
more areas being reviewed. There is also an upper limit, or point of
diminishing returns, in the size of these refined teams. This appears to
be about 9 members, including the moderator. The optimum size appears to
be 7 members.

The preliminary forecast is presented to the individual members of
the team a week or two prior to their formal meeting. This gives them
time to give serious thought to the preliminary forecast and in some
cases to look up specific references in journals, or to refresh their
memories in other ways. The meetings are held in a conference room with
a minimum of distractions. A tape recorder can be used to make a permanent record of all comments made during the T/F refinement session. A
blackboard can be used for individuals to present ideas graphically and
a Polaroid camera with colored film can record these spontaneous graphic
concepts which may employ colored chalk.

It has been found that if the group is kept to a small size most of
the objections to forecasting through committee discussion are almost
totally eliminated. The greater problem is the influence of a very
prestigious member, or a participant with strong and overriding personality. This influence can be reduced by the tactful influence of the
moderator who will shift the discussion to other subjects or direct
specific questions to some of the less vocal specialists.

The third meeting usually reflects a consensus of opinion among the
experts very similar to that noted by Helmer and Gordon in their Delphi
technique. After the final meeting, the moderator prepares a draft of
the final refined technological forecast and copies of the draft are
sent to each of the team members who can then make suggested changes or
modifications. The moderator then incorporates these written corrections
into the final document projecting foreseeable trends in a specific or
related area.

Technological forecasting can be a very stimulating intellectual
activity with significant appeal to knowledgeable scientists and engineers.
If it is properly directed, these people will give their very best efforts, and will put in more outside time and reflection in the activity
than they normally allot to less stimulating tasks. Motivation of the
team members and the group dynamics involved are important areas to be
investigated by the behavioral scientists who will unquestionably make a
very great contribution to the emerging art of synthesis forecasting using
small refinement teams.

The final T/F document is an integrated forecast with a consensus
summary of the forecasting teams final conclusions. It contains:

1. Long term state-of-the-are projections at alternate R.D.T. and
E. funding levels.

2. Descriptions of possible Hahn-Strassmann point discoveries.

3. Identification of key applied research objectives and the human,
economic and facilities requirements that may permit their near-term
realization.

4. Identification of possible synergistic relationships between
technologies.

5. Brings to light relatively unknown physical and biological
phenomena that may offer basic research promise of Hahn-Strassmann point
discoveries.

6. Defines basic research areas where increased support may result
in Hahn-Strassmann point discoveries.

7. Clarifies supposed natural barriers in order to determine if they
are really fundamental limitations.

Ralph C. Lenz has stressed the importance of published T/F documents:
"Forecasting is valueless for comparison with actual events unless it is
recorded. The recorded technological forecast is a most effective warning that change is necessary. In contrast, a plan with an unrecorded
forecast may be adhered to in spite of changing circumstances since the
divergence of actual events from the forecast is not detected. The recorded forecast is also useful as a standard in reviewing major commitments at critical points. Divergence of events from those forecasts may
be a signal for the avoidance of further commitments or the termination
of the action."

In addition to being reproduced and distributed, *decision makers
must believe the contents of published forecasts*. They must consider
the scientific and technological objectives as being possible, economically feasible and worthwhile. This acceptance will permit advanced T/F
to be used effectively in preparing official long range action plans.
T/F must be effectively integrated with policy and objectives of both
government agencies and private organizations.

The full integration of advanced T/F into all branches of government
and industry concerned with science and technology will be of immense
benefit to the national space program. There were excellent T/F documents on achievable space accomplishments published in the late 40's
and the early 50's by Wernher von Braun, Arthur C. Clark, Willy Ley and
others. These forecasts are the reality of contemporary astronautics;
nevertheless it required the competitive threat of Sputnik to cause
political and military leaders to acknowledge the vital importance of s
space exploration and to realize that it was not science fiction but an
environment that man would soon explore.

In the mid-50's, the complacency of American leaders stemmed from
technological *naivety*. The supreme irony is the fact that we are again
drifting into a comparable position of inaction. The importance of future
planetary exploration is not accepted. The advantages of lunar-base
operations and research is not understood. The vital role of future
manned orbital military systems is discounted from a "cost effectiveness"
standpoint, despite the fact that all competent T/F specialists, American
and Russian, agree that the nation that controls space from low orbit to
synchronous orbit will be in a position to rule the world. In summary,
both civilian and military space programs are being severly neglected.

The solution to our current space dilemma is to educate members of
congress, government officials, corporation executives, the entire scientific community and the general public. They must become converts who
believe that our manifest destiny is to explore and permanently occupy
this new environment. Published T/F documents can play a vital role in
this educational process and some initial progress can be reported.

Present space operations are extremely expensive and much T/F refinement must be devoted to exploring the technological answers to the "cost
effectiveness barrier". Attention must be given to reuseable launch systems and reducing ground support requirements. The Hahn-Strassmann point
has been passed in the nuclear rocket and the supersonic combustion

ramjet. These advanced propulsion systems can become operational in the
1970's with proper T/F direction and implementation. The new high-
modulous filament-composite materials can reduce the mass fraction of
reuseable transports, permitting large earth-to-orbit payloads. Guidance,
on-board-checkout and systems reliability can be outlined through synthesis T/F.

In space propulsion for economic orbit-to-orbit transport must be
subject to careful T/F scrutiny, including techno-economic tradeoff
studies. Each advanced in-space propulsion approach is likely to meet
certain requirements. The ion engine, nuclear rocket, and more advanced
concepts such as gaseous core and nuclear-pulse systems, can greatly reduce the cost of space operations. A long-range T/F analysis indicates
that controlled thermonuclear-fusion propulsion may permit colonization
of the entire solar system in the 21st century. These advanced possibilities are still in the science-fiction domain. T/F can bring them
into the necessary perspective so that related R & D programs can be
started. T/F can supply information needed for political and economic
justification.

Space T/F in the life sciences is also necessary. The detailed requirements of reliable life-support systems must be better defined. The
answers to behavioral problems in alien environments must be understood
well in advance of final spacecraft design. T/F must be used to justify
research in some of the more daring bioastronautic proposals. Is human
hibernation possible? What would be its effect on space logistics and
psychological problems? Is a modified cyborg approach desirable? To
what extent should electronic prothesis be surgically implanted? The
technology transfer prospects of bioastronautics will be an important T/F
contribution in justifying large space budgets.

The readers can supply many additional T/F subjects from their own
experience. Electronic miniaturization, energy conversion, communication
technology, and systems integration are but a few of the areas that must
be included in imaginative space T/F.

The full implementation of space T/F can insure our country of a
glorious future. It can provide the challenge that will keep alive our
pioneer spirit, a mental attitude which must be nourished by the availability of new frontiers to explore and colonize. Space exploration may
even provide humanity with a lasting substitute for war. Man is the
master of his own destiny. If we learn to forecast our technological
future successfully, then we are more likely to take the timely steps into deep space that will prevent America from following Rome's pattern of
decline and fall.

Mr. Prehoda has argued that technological
forecasting should be used to accelerate
the progress of technology, by choosing for
emphasis those areas with the highest potential payoff. But how is the payoff to be
determined? And of all the possible technological projects, with their associated
costs and payoffs, which should be selected
for emphasis? There are the kinds of
questions Dr. Cetron addresses in the following essay.

TECHNOLOGICAL FORECASTING FOR THE MILITARY MANAGER

MARVIN J. CETRON

*Forecasting International Ltd., 9324 Convento Terrace,
Fairfax, Virginia 22030, U.S.A.*

BACKGROUND

Over the past five years, both government and industry have become
fascinated with the potential of technological forecasting as an aid in
planning R&D budgets. As laboratories expanded and budgets grew, managers found that many of the traditional ways of allocating their resources of men and money seemed inadequate. But most attempts to build
better allocation systems foundered on two basic questions: Which research areas are most likely to be the source of significant technical
breakthroughs? Which breakthrough are most likely to bring an important new development?

The realization that technological forecasting methods could answer
these questions was catching hold slowly when many R&D planners were
rudely shaken by a new reality: a leveling-off or even a cutback in
most government-sponsored research efforts. With NASA's post-Apollo
projects whittled back, the United States DOD research budgets cut extensively, and other usually expanding budgets on a shorter rein, the
need to make hard choices in funding became more critical than ever.
Now many planners are turning to technological forecasting to help them
make their difficult selections.

As a result of previous presentations to the NATO Defense Research
Group, on techniques for making technological forecasts, I have received many requests for further information. However, most of these
requests were not for information on how to make technological forecasts,
but for information on how technological forecasts, once made, could be
integrated into R&D planning efforts. In this paper, I will explain
some of the approaches being examined within the United States Department of the Navy, as well as some of the directions being actively explored in US industry. However, you should keep in mind that this field
is still in an evolutionary phase and the work being done in any one
organization is sufficiently unique that it cannot easily be adapted for
use in others. At best, what is being done can provide many helpful
hints for planners grappling with the difficulties of using technological forecasts in their own allocation problems.

It is vital to remember that a technological forecast is not a
picture of what the future will bring. Instead, it is a prediction,
with a level of confidence, in a given time frame, of a technical
achievement that could be expected for a given level of budgetary and
manpower support.

The foundation underlying technological forecasting is the tenet that individual R&D events are susceptible to influence. The time at which they occur - if they can occur at all - can be modulated significantly by regulating the resources allocated to them. Another basic tenet of technological forecasting is the belief that many futures are possible and that the paths toward these futures can be *mapped*.

In use, a technological forecast can be looked at from two vantage points. One, in the present, gives the forecast user a view which shows in path that technological progress will probably take if it is not consciously influenced. In addition, the user will see critical branch points in the road - the situation where alternative futures are possible. He will also gain a greater understanding of the price of admission to those branching paths.

The second vantage point is in the future. The user selects or postulates a technical situation he desires. Looking backward from the point, he can then discern the obstacles that must be overcome to achieve the result he wants. Once again, he is brought up against the hard realities of what he must do to achieve a desired result. As one user has said: "The process substitutes forecasting for forecrastination."

All currently available techniques for making technological forecasts have one common aspect: they depend on the use of historical data. There is no provision in them for the systematic introduction of management plans and actions. To take these into account, the forecaster must make his own intuitive judgements about the actions of managers and decision-makers. There is some work being done on more sophisticated methods of forecasting, using systems analysis and mathematical modeling. Basic to these methods is the interaction of the technical state of the art with human awareness of economic, social and geopolitical needs. The technical inputs are formulated by the methods currently in use, and then examined for nontechnical feasibility. However, these methods have not yet been developed to the point of practical application.

PUTTING FORECASTS TO WORK

In most cases, a manager does not have a total system to work with. Instead, he has the results of trend extrapolations or other regular technological forecasting projections. How does he use these date? While there are many approaches, the following is one which the Navy Department is examining to determine which techniques can best help decide which R&D projects to fund.

We begin with a technical planning flow chart (Fig. 1) that shows the "shredding out" of all the bits and pieces that comprise the makeup of a new vehicle. Assume that we have a technological forecast for each and every parameter of the shred-out. The forecasts, at each level of the breakdown, are the probable paths that various technologies will take. Armed with this type of data, a meaningful discourse can ensue between the user and producer. For a given set of operational requirements and performance characteristics called for by the user, the technical planners can respond with data that tell the user by what alternative means his needs can be satisfied, and when he can expect these to be accomplished. Many of the trade-offs - between steam, diesel, and nuclear energy, for example - become clear.

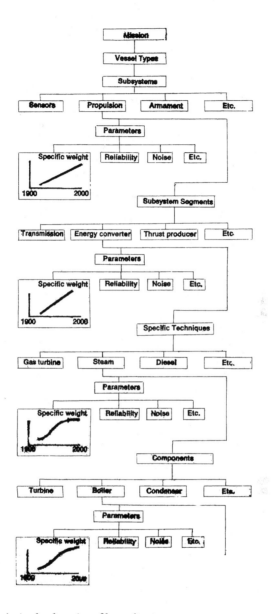

Fig. 1. Technical planning flow chart.

Operations officers, however, are not usually quite so acquiscent
in accepting what a planner sees ahead. When faced with a military
threat, or an anticipated threat, they want an effective answer to that
threat by a specific date. The same holds true if they wish to create
a new force of their own. In these situations, planners are taking a
vantage point at some time in the future and are trying to discover
if they will have the technology they need by that time.

Quite likely an examination of the technological forecasts to that point in time will reveal that the users are not likely to get what they want. Now, this is useful information in itself, and represents an approach that is not yet widely used in industry.

However, this view of the technological forecasting task is not the only one. There is the question of which path we should take to achieve result. By deciding on our needs in the future and looking at the forecasts, we can spot the principal obstacles standing in our way, and the magnitude of those obstacles. The inference is clear: If the given goal is to be achieved in a given time, the efforts must be applied in the areas containing the major obstacles. Or, we can settle for something less with clear knowledge of what that something less will be. Often, this analysis will show that two or more paths may be taken to achieve the needed or acceptable capabilities. The point here is that an environment of flexible choice is engendered - choices of which the user was not previously aware. A truly comprehensive technological forecast is backed up not only by material and data which were used in generating the specific forecasts but also by supplementary analysis of various subfactors that could influence each technological forecast. Forecasts like these help indicate the future posture of an enemy or competitor. While you don't know what he *will* do, you at least have a better idea of what he *could* or *could not* do.

MECHANICS OF DECISION-MAKING

Now let's turn to an example and see how a specific decision can be analyzed, based on the forecasting techniques utilized at the Annapolis Division of Naval Ships Research and Development Center. Forecasts for ship propulsion systems are given in terms of specific weight, reliability, noise, etc. The next level of consideration takes us into the area of subsystem segments - transmission, energy converter, thrust producer, etc. Each of these key into an associated set of parameters which, in turn, key into specific forecasts. In this fashion, we can work our way down the chart, (Fig. 1), eventually going into any degree of detail we wish.

This information is used for very practical decisions. Marine gas turbines, for example, have a tremendous potential for development. The possibilities for high-power, lightweight, compact power plants are unmatched in any other type of unit. These characteristics are particularly vital for powering new-concept vessels much as hydrofoils and air-cushion craft. In the last few years, there has been a rapid growth in the horsepower capacity of gas turbine units. Engines as large as 43,000 horsepower have been built, and units exceeding 50,000 horsepower are projected. This growth trend will probably continue but at a lesser rate as limitations of mechanical, thermal and ducting size are approached. However, much larger power outputs will be built by using multiple gas generators to drive a single turbine engine. Power outputs as high as 150,000 horsepower have already been attained by this method. The R&D manager's problem is to decide which aspects of turbine development are most critical.

The development trends for the specific weight, volume, and fuel consumption for a simple cycle gas turbine are shown in the graphs (Fig. 2). In all of these the trend correlation (lead-follow relationship) was used in the study. Aircraft gas-turbine technology has been the

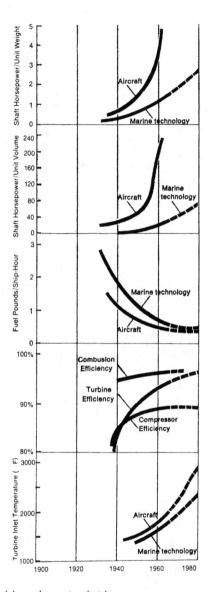

Fig. 2.   Gas turbine characteristics.

leader not only because of the greater aircraft speed payoff, but also
because the marine environment led to problems of corrosion. Now that
materials and other problems are being overcome, the curves are coming
together - the aircraft experience gives some indication of what can
be expected in future naval turbines.

As shown in the efficiency graph in Fig. 2, the compressor combustion, and turbine efficiency have reached a plateau according to growth -

analogy study. Any future improvement will be limited. Consequently, these components efficiencies will have an insignificant effect on future engine characteristics. Recent improvements, moreover, have resulted from an increase in the compressor-pressure ratio. But any further increase will be small. Because of improvements in blade loading, compressors are now designed to an optimum pressure rate determined by turbo inlet temperature. And this blade loading, which has enabled engines to obtain higher pressures with fewer stages, appears to be approaching a limit.

This combination of forecasts shows that the addition of more heat energy within the same basic engine configuration – the major contributing factor to recent engine improvement – is likely to be the key factor in future improvement. Extrapolation of the curve to temperatures in excess of 2500° F is based on laboratory tests in which operating temperatures as high as 4000° F have been achieved – another trend correlation forecast.

As a result of this forecasting approach we now know where our R&D efforts should be concentrated. These are the high payoffs:

1. Cooling of turbine blades and other components in high-temperature ambients. This will allow higher turbine inlet temperature.

2. New materials and protective coatings for these high-ambient components. This will increase high-temperature capabilities by increasing resistance to high-temperature oxidation and sulfidation. An increased resistance to thermal fatigue and creep is also required.

3. Improved materials, designs, and fabrication techniques for regenerative gas turbines to reduce their cost, weight, and bulk.

4. Further application and adaptation of aircraft gas turbines and technologies to ships.

5. Attempts to improve efficiency of combustion, compressor, and turbine.

6. Attempts to increase significantly the blade loading or compressor-pressure ratio if accompanied by major design changes.

THE OVERALL PICTURE

Up to this point we have been discussing the technological forecasting needed for one problem in a laboratory. But any organization has many such problems. Here the question becomes one of allocation of resources of men, money, and materials. The evaluation scene therefore shifts from the technical specialist to the department manager, the head of research, and the overall planners. The forecast data must be fitted into their overall planning approach if it is to be really useful.

When the management problems are simple, a decision-maker can examine the various factors he must consider with relative ease. One man, such as the hermit in a cave, the individual homeowner, the small businessman, or the teacher in a one-room school, may be able to interrelate all the necessary information and succeed in his endeavors.

As the management scope becomes larger and the complexity of problems increases, more and different factors must be considered to reach a decision. Soon, staff and management procedures are needed to assist in all phases of management. Eventually, the point is reached where any

one decision affects many facets of the operation; all efforts become
interrelated to an alarming degree.

Increasing complexities are particularly true with programs or projects which must operate within a fixed government or corporation resource ceiling. Choices must be made on alternative approaches, specifically, which efforts should proceed and which should be dropped or de-
layed. Since numerous efforts are interrelated in time, resources required, purpose and possible technical transfer one to another, choices must
be made with consideration of the total effect. Whether is be a manu-
facturer, a service industry director, government administrator, or university professor, every manager seeks the greatest payoff for resource
investments.

What alternatives does a manager have for developing resource-allo-
cation approaches? The resource allocation problem is usually too big
to keep in one man's head and often inputs come from levels completely
outside of his control. Hundreds of inputs can be involved when the alternatives are examined in depth.

A familiar resource allocation approach is termed the *squeaking
wheel* process. One can cut resources from every area (one can be sophisticated and cut some areas more than others) then wait and see
which area complains the most. On the basis of the loudest and most
insistent squeaking, the manager can then restore some of the resources
previously withdrawn until he reaches his ceiling budget.

Another common approach develops the minimum noise level and results
in fewer sqeaks by allocating this year's resources in just about the
same manner as last year. The budget perturbations are minimized and the
status quo maintained. If this *level funding* apprach is continued very
long within a rapidly changing technological field, the company, group,
or government agency will end up in serious trouble.

An effortless version of the preservation of management security approach to resource allocation seeks to perpetuate the *Glorious Past*.
Last year, or the year before, or perhaps several years ago, a division
or organization had a very successful project, therefore why not fund
the unit for the next five years on any projects that they advocate?
The premise is "once successful, always successful." This method really
means that no analysis should be made of the proposed project or its usefulness; instead, projects will be assigned resources solely upon the basis of past record of an individual or organization.

Still another way to allocate resources is called the *white charger*
technique. Here the various departments come dashing in to top management with multi-color graphs, handouts, and well-rehearsed presentations.
If they impress the decision-maker, they are rewarded with increased resources. Often the best speaker or the last man to brief the boss wins
the treasure.

Finally, consider the *committee approach*, which frees the manager
from resource allocation decisions. The committees tell the manager to
increase, decrease, or leave all allocations as they are. A common danger is that the committee may not have enough actual experience in the
organization or sufficient information upon which to base its recommendations. If the committee is ad hoc or from outside the organization,
the members can also avoid responsibility in not having to live through
the risky process of implementing their recommendations.

Obviously, the described allocation methods are neither scientific
nor objective, though they are utilized quite extensively. These naive
approaches point up the need of the manager and his staff for an aid to
bring information into a form upon which judgement may be applied. It
is a common experience for an organization to have numerous reports on
specific technical subjects which recommended increased resources for
the particular area. But the direct use of this data only compounds
the manager's problem when he tries to allocate resources among the many
technical areas. If he is operating under a fixed budget ceiling, to
increase funding for one technical area requires that either one or more
technical areas must be correspondingly decreased.

TECHNOLOGICAL RESOURCE ALLOCATION SYSTEM

A more sophisticated alternative approach involves the use of staff
or specialists in operations research. Information they assemble can be
used to significantly assist managerial judgement. This is the point
where quantitative evaluation techniques enter the picture. Each major
aspect of a program can be examined, first separately and then as it is
interrelated to competing factors. Items such as timeliness, cost utility or payoff, confidence level or risk, personnel, facilities, etc.,
can be evaluated by specialists in each field and the total picture made
available as a basis for decision. Greater payoff areas can be identified and problems can be highlighted. Inputs can be accurately recorded,
made clearly visible and analyzed for assisting the final decision.

The use of quantitative techniques permits input factors and possible
outcome to be reexamined readily and different managerial emphasis applied. The manager can still hedge his "allocation selections" by allocating resources through such criteria as increased resources to previously successful groups, backing a high-risk effort - i.e., a high cost
project with slim chances of success which might yield gigantic results.
The decision-maker can incorporate any desired additional criteria - such
as the politics of selection, competitive factors, or technological bar-
biers.

The question now becomes one of allocation of the resources of men,
money, and materials. Fig. 3, the long-range planning diagram, which
is really a broad allocation diagram, shows the interactions of numerous
managers from the technical specialist to the department manager, the
head of research, and the corporate planners. The data must be fitted
into an overall planning approach if it is to be really useful. Corpor-
rate goals are the main topic and occupy the central position in the
chart. In order to establish corporate goals, the preliminary steps
of systems analysis, needs analysis, and deficiency analysis must be
accomplished. After the goals and technical objectives are established,
technology assessment and R&D Programming take place to complete the
R&D resources allocation process. Each of these steps will be explained in greater depth.

System Analysis

Corporate policy must be considered and involves philosophic and
strategy questions, including these: Shall I be the industry leader?
Shall I keep abreast of the industry technically and see if a major
market develops? In the overall environment, competitors' actions
must be followed closely, but there are other factors such as interest
rates, business expectation, economic forecasts, etc. to be identified.

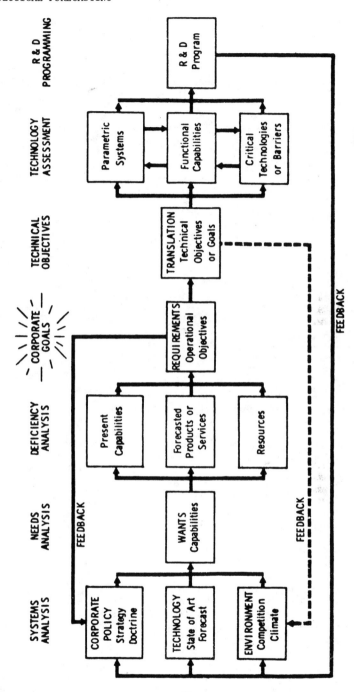

10
Fig. 3.   Long range R&D planning.

Fig. 3 viewed as the corporate planning chart, shows a recommended organization of considerations.

The technology forecasting element acts as a catalyst in setting and implementing overall corporate goals. At present only a handful of the largest corporations are really utilizing their full corporate technical potential. The next question is how to relate the technological forecasts with appraisal in this total picture. A discussion of the numerous appraisal methods would be along story in itself. For example, all systems employed by the Department of Defense utilize three major factors in the appraisal or normative forecasting process: military utility, technical feasibility, and financial acceptability. Each of these factors is amenable to quantification and can be fitted into a model which compares the value of each component project or system. Due to the complexity of the analysis, it is necessary to program the job on a computer to get usable information quickly. It must be remembered, however, that these computer processes are simply a tool to aid the decision-maker; the machine merely arranges the material in accordance with his instructions so that he can quickly focus his attention on those areas which require his special knowledge and judgment.

The environment (competition, climate) also must be considered, and include such questions as: Who are the competitors? What unique skills, products, or finances do these competitors possess? What is the industry-wide climate? What is the industry-wide climate? Will the industry demand continue to expand rapidly, will there be a sudden drop in demand, or will a leveling of demand be expected. The factors considered under the systems analysis allow the needs (wants) as well as the unique or strong capabilities of the firm to be identified.

Need Analysis

Analysis of the wants or desirable areas of growth for the firm is equally as important as defining the areas where no growth or decline is expected.

The national of international economy provides the broadest scope for analysis of the needs for the firm's products or services. The stage of development in the country, the requirements from related industries, the availability and cost of capital and governmental controls may all require attention for the process of determining what the firm "wants" to do.

The industry share-of-the-market for the firm relates directly to its volume. That is, in an industry of rapid growth the individual firm may grow while remaining constant relative to its competitors. Conversely, the share-of-the-market may need to be greatly increased to remain at a level stage in a declining industry.

Finally, the desire of the firm and of the individual groups within the firm can be assessed. However, these desires may not be attainable within the capability of the firm. Thus, the wants need to be balanced against the firm's capabilities.

Deficiency Analysis

After the wants of the organization have been established, the capabilities available must be delineated in order that areas of deficiency can be identified. Ordinarily, the present capabilities of an organization will be known, but often effort is required by management to obtain a comprehensive statement of its technological capabilities in terms of men, money, and machines. Because we are dealing with futures, the products and services such as new manufacturing methods, new materials, and advanced skills that are forecasted to be available must also be carefully identified. Other resources available to the organization will also be important information. Skills or manufacturing processes or equipment, etc. may exist that could be available from outside the organization when and if required.

By identifying and analyzing the present capabilities, forecasted products and services along with other resources available, the deficiencies and excesses will become evident. The analysis now permits management to focus upon realistic corporate goals.

Corporate Goals

The most important phase of the resource allocation system may now be brought into focus - the corporate goals (objectives). These goals may be viewed by top management from the wants (desires or needs) of the organization which have been carefully considered for feasibility against the present or potential capabilities of the organization. Several passes through the analysis described above usually are required before acceptable goals are achieved by top management.

These corporate goals will be translated into requirements for performance of the organization, or as operational objectives.

Technical Objectives

The idea of applying quantitative approaches to resource allocation has too long been suspect by management. Currently, both industry and government are seeking tangible improvements in the results from use of available resources. Economy drives and or cost/benefit analysis have resulted in pared budgets with the need more critical than ever to make hard choices among alternative programs. The application of objective measurements to resource assignments has too long been classified as visionary and impractical.

For example, how does a corporation decide whether its allocation this year for research and technology is adequate? And how does it decide the right balance between the research and development or manufacturing projects?

A prime example of lack of quantitative data exists in the area of assessing technological effort. Querying the scientist or engineer and requesting a justification of his selection of a program or a task (including projected benefits to a mission or product-oriented organization) has often been construed as an assault against the scientific professionals' prestige and prerogatives. Today, scientists and engineers are beginning to realize that they are accepted at the highest organization levels and that one of the signs of this ascendancy is their high visibility and responsibility to the interrogation of criteria and rational judgments. The technical managers intuition can no longer be accepted as infallible and beyond managerial review.

Several project evaluation and selection techniques have as their basis a belief in the efficacy and acceptance of Bayesian statistics and theories of probability. Bayesians believe that it is correct to quantify feelings about uncertainty in terms of subjectively assessed numerical probabilities. Thus, assessments are made of probabilities for events that determine the profitability or utility of alternative actions open to the decision-maker.

For example, there is a necessity to assess the criterion of whether a piece of research is technically feasible (Technological Forecasts) or what is the probability that it will be successfully accomplished (level of confidence criterion). Bayesian theory believes that it is possible for an "expert" in the field being assessed to assign a figure of merit or "subjective" probability number that the event will actually occur. This theory states that on this very subject matter an expert can assign a "subjective" probability number from a scale, for example, between 0 and 10. Men of considerable experience in a field usually have no difficulty in utilizing a Bayesian probability scale. In a like manner, other criteria, such as the utility of the research to the objectives of the organization, or relevance to desired priority systems or corporation products, are assessed (criterion of utility).

The use of Bayesian subjective probabilities makes feasible the incorporation into the decision process, in a formal and visible way, many of the subjective and objective criteria and variables previously taken into account by the decision-maker informally and without visibility.

The probability assignment, a number between 0 and 10 to each facet, factor, criterion, or parameter inherent to a rational decision, reflects the degree of belief held by the individual expert(s) that the above objective will be met.

Thus the experience, knowledge of the subject, and judgment of the various experts are summarized by the subjective probabilities that they assign against the respective criteria. The final or top decision-maker then has a clear view of the alternatives and can use the results of the probability assignments of the different experts. A computer can be used to summarize the choices or probabilities of the experts. The computer can also be used to determine "consequences" if the probability assignments are changed or if the final decision-maker adds new information or weighting factors, etc.

Advocates of allocation and selection procedures are accused of assuming that the myriad of quantitative estimates of scientific relevance, importance, feasibility and the like should and can be collected and manipulated. Apparently the academic community also believes in the above assumption. For example, in the field of education, the university admission policy is based on a "myriad of quantitative estimates."

Mr. Robert Freshman, one of the U.S. Air Force Laboratory planners who was previously a professional educator, relates the following example: High school students are admitted to universities based on the quantitative judgements of teacher grades as the key criterion. These teachers grade about 5 subjects a year, for 4 years of high school - thus, 20 teachers' judgments. Different teachers, different subjects, different tests, different subject matter taken in high schools throughout the nation, are fused into one. Teacher opinions on how to grade, biases and prejudgments, oral recitations, grades on nonstandardized, unstructured subject matter and tests are all injected into the above conglomeration to form the individual teacher's final grade in one subject.

High school grades for the four years are averaged to come up with one number - the high school average - the *magic number* which has great influence in college admission. More miraculous is that there is a good, positive correlation between this magic number and success in college. It is recognized that this "quantitative estimate" of many judgments is the best single criterion or indicator of success in *college*; but again it is just an aid to the decision-maker. The personal interview, college boards, or extra curricular activities also effect his judgment prior to making a final decision.

Opinions and judgments can be and should be weighted by every decision-maker in his final decision. Several quantitative techniques gather and summarize the opinions and judgments to enable the final decision-maker (like the university dean of admissions utilizing teacher judgments) to visualize and weigh, as one input to his decision, the judgments of numerous people on diverse factors.

Two main points on quantitative decision making should be emphasized:

(a) The quantitative management techniques discussed *do not make decisions*, but provide a basis of information upon which decisions can be made.

(b) A validity check cannot be made since once the resources are allocated, the plan becomes self-fulfilling.

Subsystem Analysis or Technology Assessment

Assessment of technology or subsystem analysis is employed to answer the question: which, when and how many resources should be allocated among the alternative projects: Since the topic is multi-faceted it is necessary to draw information from a variety of sources including operations research, project selection techniques, and technological forecasting.

Technology assessment is not official jargon. The expression "assessment of technology" is not found listed in the table of contents or indexes of texts on management. Nor is it identified and found in the general literature of management or in official planning, programming and policy documents of the government agencies.

Assessment is commonly considered to mean "setting a value to." Assessement of technology, then, means setting a value of technology. Technologies include areas of special knowledge such as gas turbines, diesels, thermionics, thermoelectrics, fuel cells, and energy conversion as opposed to the areas of science which include items such as alloy theory, surface physics, cryogenics, and magnetism. The kinds or measures of value attributed to technologies will be discussed later. Also, it can be demonstrated that the nature of the assessment of technology depends on who assesses, why the assessment is performed, and the nature of the technology, itself.

Who Assesses Technology and Why - Or For What Purpose?

Intuitively, nearly everyone assesses technology at some time, for some purpose, and to some degree of sophistication. The "man on the street" for example may essentially assess the aggregates of the technologies of color versus black and white television. He may consider the collective value of parameters such as cost, picture quality, repair frequency, and pressure from his wife in order to choose which, if either, to buy. That nearly everyone has different values was pointed out by William D. Guth and Renato Tagiuri which emphasized the following points:

The personal values that businessmen and others have can be usefully classified as theoretical, economic, aesthetic, social, political, and religious.

The values that are most important to an executive have profound influence on his strategic decisions.

Managers and employees often are unaware of the values they possess and also tend to misjudge the values of others.

The executive who will take steps to better understand his own values and other men's values can gain an important advantage in developing workable and well-supported policies.

Since the assessment of technology is unavoidable, the real issue is whether this assessment will be made in a rational manner, or whether the assessment will be left to chance or done only implicitly. Once the issue is stated in this manner, it seems almost obvious that the assessment should be made explicitly and rationally. To the extent that rationality can replace intuition, it should be given the chance to do so.

The U.S. Navy is currently investigating one such rational approach to allocating resources to technology, through explicit assignment of numerical values to technological efforts. One part of the assessment involves the importance of the technology area to naval warfare. This assessment is made by staff agencies most qualified to evaluate the military value of technology, on the assumption that it is technically feasible. Another part of the assessment involves the cost of the technology. In fact, values are calculated for three different cost levels. The final part of the assessment, and the most important from the standpoint of this paper, is the assessment of technical feasibility.

This assessment is in fact a technological forecast. It is made by those responsible for the technological program, and who are therefore best qualified to make this assessment. The assessment is expressed as a probability of success, that is, a probability that the program can meet its technical goals.

These three parts are then combined into a single numerical score, obtained by multiplying the military value by the probability of success. This product is then divided by the cost of the program. This final score can then be used to rank individual projects, so that resources can be allocated to those with the highest scores. In this way, a technological forecast can be included in the assessment of a technology, and in an explicit fashion. The ability to make explicit use of a quantitative technological forecast, of course, depends on the fact that the other assessment can also be made quantitatively. If cost and value are not assessed in quantitative terms, the quantitative forecast may be of little help.

CONCLUSION

I am well aware of many of the omissions and weaknesses of these quantitative selection or resource allocation techniques. It should be stressed again that they were not intended to yield decision, but rather information which would faciliate decision. Indeed, these techniques are merely thinking structures to force methodical, meticulous consideration of all the factors involved in resource allocation. *Data* plus *analysis* yields *information*. *Information* plus *judgment* yields *decisions*.

Data + Analysis = Information

Information + Judgment = Decision

I am firmly convinced that if I had to choose between any machine and the human brain, I would select the brain. The brain has a marvelous system that learns from experience and an uncanny way of pulling out the salient factors or rejecting useless information. It is wrong to say that one must select intuitive experience over analysis or minds over machines; really they are *not* alternatives, they complement each other. Used together, they yield results far better than if used individually.

A close look at a few "facts" concerning the quantitative resource allocation methods shows these approaches to be merely experimental management techniques. The fact that a computer or an adding machine may be used to faciliate data handling should, in no way distract from the basic fact that human subjective inputs are the foundation of these systems. Accurate human calculation, as opposed to use of a computer for the calculations of all the interrelationships considered would not alter the basic principles of these management tools in any respect. Yet, I often hear the reactionary complaint that quantitative measurements cannot be applied to management processes because human judgment cannot be forsaken and machines cannot replace the seasoned experience expertise of the manager.

The real concern should be directed toward using the collective judgment of technical staffs (technological forecasts) and decision-makers in such a manner that logically sound decisions are made, greater payoff is achieved for the resources committed, and that less, not more, valuable scientific and engineering time expended. To make an incorrect decision is understandable, but to make a decision and not really know the basis for the judgment is unforgivable. The area of good resource allocation certainly must have advanced beyond this point; otherwise, a pair of dice could replace the decision-maker.

Most of the managers who design and work with information systems fully realize that technological forecasts, quantitative estimates of project value, and other aids to resource allocation are merely a planning tool — and only one of a brand new kit of advanced decision-making devices.

Even this caveat, however, does not defuse critics of the whole idea — and there are some very vocal ones around in government and business. Some of the criticism is in reaction to the fear of "mechanization" of a task felt to be rightfully in the province of human evaluation. Other critics claim that building up a logical system, computerizing the output, and quantifying what are essentially intuitive and judgment decisions may insulate some managers with a false sense of security. The validation of the process will not be continued and management responsibility will be abandoned. Another criticism stems from the use of estimates as basic figures in the analysis. This kind of objection can also be applied to decision based on "experience" and made without a quantitative approach.

Technological forecasting and systematic analysis tend to force managers to consider their resource allocation tasks more comprehensively and highlights problem areas that might easily be overlooked by more traditional approaches. However, regardless of the high degree of sophistication being attributed to these planning devices, managers should use them with caution.

The preceding essays have discussed the use of
technological forecasting from the standpoint
of projecting future capabilities, and determining which of those should actually be
achieved. The following essay presents
another approach, that of determining future
requirements, then deciding what must be done
now to permit those requirements to be satisfied when the proper time comes.

INDUSTRIAL IMPLICATIONS OF TECHNOLOGICAL FORECASTING*

WILLIAM L. SWAGER

*Department of Economics and Information Research, Battelle Memorial Insti-
tute, Columbus Labs., Columbus Ohio, 43201, U.S.A.*

Modern management depends more and more on improved technology, yet
research daily grows more complex and costly. Rocketing R & D budgets,
even at this moment, attack well-established strongholds of fiscal policy
in industry. Is there any way out? May the solution not lie in improved
R & D management?

Much can undoubtedly be done to improve efficiency and creativity
"within the lab" [1, 2, 3]. However, serious problems at which might be
called the "top management-laboratory" interface must be solved. It is
here that a clear-cut business strategy is most needed. Today, diffuse
strategy leads to ill-defined efforts in the laboratory. Insight and understanding of future trends of technology needed for strategy formulation
is filtered or distorted before reaching policy-making levels.

It is absolutely essential that the log jam of problems at this top
management-laboratory interface be well and truly broken. Ways must be
found to forecast technological advances and to spell out their business
implications. Top policy-makers must be clearly briefed. They will
challenge, discuss, examine, and re-examine. When they come to decide a
crucial course, they will have a realistic strategy. R & D will know
where it is going, and why.

This paper will examine how technological forecasts fit the needs of
business executives and research managers alike. It will attempt to define what constitutes a useful technological forecast.

NEED FOR TECHNOLOGICAL FORECASTING

Today, few executives in American industry acknowledge clearly and
specifically their need for forecasts of technology. Fewer are willing
to admit that such forecasts may be of practical value. Still fewer recognize that every investment decision made by industry today is made
with an assumed or estimated, conscious or unconscious, good or bad technological forecast. At the same time, none deny the impact on business
of the rapid rate of technological change.

*Reprinted from: *Decision Making Criteria for Capital Expenditures*,
ed. A. Lesser, Jr., Engineering Economist, Stevens Instit. of Tech.,
Hoboken, N.J., 1966.

They tend to agree with James Bright, of the Harvard Business School,
who maintains there are seven important tides of technological change [4]
These are: (1) increased transportation capability, (2) increased mastery
of energy, (3) extension and control of life - both animate and inanimate,
(4) increased ability to alter the characteristics of materials, (5) extension of sensory capabilities, (6) mechanization of physical activities,
and (7) mechanization of intellectual activities.

Bright argues convincingly that these tides of technological change
are great forces affecting the future of every business in this country.
For example, he forecasts: Competition from distant geographical areas and
from nontraditional and unexpected fields will increase, and the competitive life span of many products will decline.

Although most businessmen agree with these reasonable generalizations,
they have questions to ask. Their questions include: How can such forecasts be related to the future of my company? How do they affect the
profitability of our present plant and equipment? How do they affect the
profitability of my company's present product lines? How can they be used
to identify opportunities for new products? How can detailed forecasts
be made that are meaningful to my business? These are all good questions,
and forecasters must give good answers to R & D management and to top
management.

Forecasts of technology can have little meaning unless they are detailed and specific to a particular company, and most company managers
simply do not believe that such valid practical forecasts are possible.
There are several reasons why businessmen have this attitude. First, most
successful businessmen are "successful" because they have been - in the
best sense of the word - opportunists. They have adjusted quickly to
change and have made change serve their changed aims. They have always
moved fast and never waited for formal forecasts. Second, they have probably been snowed under by prognostications of technical changes that
could affect them, and have found out later how few of these prophesies
were fulfilled. Third, they have known disenchantment when the glowing
hopes fanned by a development man for a new product faded rapidly in the
marketplace. Finally, they think they have heard it all before - economic forecasts, market forecasts, weather forecasts - they are weary of
forecasters.

Not managers alone, but research men, scientists, and engineers also
doubt that technological forecasting is feasible. They resent the term
and they misunderstand it. They jump to the conclusion that technological
forecasting means predicting scientific "breakthroughs." Let it be understood that "technology" means "science in practical use," and will never
be taken to mean anything else. Let it be stated and stressed that the
terms "scientific" or "technical" are not synonymous with "technological";
that advances in technology are conditioned by economics and by the
marketplace; and that in the term "technological forecasting" there is no
inference that breakthroughs in science can be predicted. Nonetheless,
we must accept the fact that the scientific community reacts unfavorably
to the use of the term.

Moreover, scientists and engineers are trained to explore *all* technical alternatives, and particularly those having apparent technical
novelty. There are more alternatives to pursue than money to provide.
That is the dilemma. If technological forecasting is to have a significant role in industry, it must be useful for indicating priorities among
alternatives. But scientists and engineers consider it presumptuous to

claim that the results of research are predictable. In their view this is,
indeed, the claim of the technological forecasters.

What are the industrial implications of technological forecasting?
There is an increasingly urgent need for better estimates of future technological changes. Business planners, market planners, R & D decision-
makers, fiscal directors - all need better estimates at all stages; all
need technological forecasts. And the time will come - and come soon -
when they will cry out for them, although they are hostile now.

My thesis is that technological forecasting will be practicable and
will have a major impact on business when we place somewhat more emphasis
on the question: *What should be forecast?* and somewhat less on *What methods
should be used for forecasting?*

EXAMINING THE QUESTION: WHAT SHOULD BE FORECAST?

Two general considerations provide guidelines when we consider the
question - What should be forecast?

First, technological forecasting is mere mental gymnastics unless the
forecast is clearly presented to, and easily interpreted by, men who make
decisions. Second, the reasoning and evaluations in any forecast should
act to reinforce the confidence of decision-makers that they have chosen
the best options.

Forecasts must make sense to scientists and engineers. To do so,
forecasts must deal with the directions of possible technological progress.
The presentation of forecasts should be understandable by technical and
non-technical people alike. Not alone must it highlight technical possibilities, but it must link these with the multiplex pressures and trends
in the total environment which condition the imminent acceptance of these
new possibilities.

Technical plausibility and an economic rationale for "utility" are
essential parts of the forecasting process. It simply will not do to
hand in a time-series or some simple statistical model without justification or explanation.

It may be well to turn now to some historical examples to see whether
or not we can gain additional insight into the question: What should be
forecast? We will look back to see how certain decisions in the past were
affected by forecasts, and we will attempt to determine what should have
been forecast.

After World War II, hundreds of millions of dollars were spent on
several dozen processes for the "direct reduction" of iron ore. The goal
in all of these programs was to reduce iron ore by natural gas or pow-
dered coal to, say 90% metal, and to bypass the traditional blast furnace.
It was hoped that the product of a direct-reduction process could be
charged directly into steel-making furnaces.

We know now that no direct reduction process will, in the foreseeable future, substitute for the blast furnace on a massive scale. However, "direct reduction" will probably be used in countries like
Venezuela, Brazil, and India. In these countries ore in pellets will be
partially reduced before shipment. Transportation charges will be lower
and employment, of great value to less highly developed countries, will

be provided. Glowing claims for direct reduction were made on the assumption that no major improvement would occur in blast furnace technology.
In fact, there was spectacular improvement - the output capacity of a
furnace was increased by 300-400 percent in the last ten years. Here is
a case where a "forecast" (and I use the term loosely) was made regarding
technological progress along one avenue, without making any forecast of
progress along another. Possible new technology was compared with the
status quo of a traditional technology.

The furor over titanium in the early 50's sprang from the belief
that a new technology of titanium would develop and that there would be a
rapid acceptance of titanium and titanium alloys in high strength-to-
weight applications. Here, again, the proponents of an improved technology "forecast" general acceptance of new titanium alloys, and ignored
the likelihood that the technology of stainless steel would not stand
still.

The early days of Carlson's development of xerography provides
another example. Carlson attempted to interest every major image repro-
ducing company in his novel use of electrostatics for image transfer. Entrenched ideas about more conventional methods of image transfer prevailed
and Carlson's offer was rejected. The possibilities of technological advance along alternative paths were underestimated, overestimated, or
overlooked.

I could cite many similar examples from my work at Battelle Institute over the past 17 years when dealing with technological forecasting.
I use the term boldly because in every applied research and development
decision, forecasts of technology are made - some explicit, most implicit.
The evidence from past experience points up the importance of the question: What should be forecast?

A decision theorist has his own particular reasons for asking himself: What should be forecast? Herbert A. Simon [5] in a paper entitled
"A Framework for Decision Making," said: "If we look at the way in which
decision-making has been talked about by engineers, by psychologists, or
by organization theorists, we detect that their way of talking about the
process is strikingly different from the way it has been discussed by
economists and by statistical decision theorists. The major difference
lies in how structured the problem is when you first meet it and, in particular, how far the problem includes discovering alternatives instead of
just choosing among alternatives."

My observations of many decision-making situations in industrial research and development have convinced me that this statement is most relevant. It is more profound than is apparent. In research and development much effort must be devoted to identifying alternatives before
selecting among them. Further, there must be a mechanism for surveillance
to assure that the initial identification and selection of alternatives
was sound.

As one would infer from the popularity of the term "creativity," discovery is of prime importance. Decision theorists today, attempting to
investigate heuristic problem-solving, press into service such terms as
"perception, relationships, order and notation, redefinition, and perspective." For them, "perception" means the identification of alternatives,
and "relationships" means the placement of alternatives in a structure
formed by logical ties among them. There is theoretic justification for
technological forecasters to be concerned with discovering alternatives
as well as choosing among them.

Several practical problems have recently led us to re-examine how we have been identifying and assigning priorities to alternatives, how we have been estimating technological advance along various possible paths. We found ourselves asking two questions: What are the forces that could stimulate change and what is the likely impact of these forces on competing technologies? Attempts to answer these questions have led us to the structuring of two graphic models that, thus far, have proved useful.

DEFINING AREAS OF SIGNIFICANT CHANGE

In a recent program we examined packaging technology in an attempt to isolate and identify the role of coatings in packaging and to predict how this role might changes in the future. The problem is complex. It involves many materials - metals, glass, paper and paperboard, and plastics. It also embraces a wide variety of natural and synthetic coating materials and methods, and a virtually unlimited number of packaging designs and applications. An unstructured search through this labyrinth of detail had little value. Attempts to identify a few overall performance parameters which might be forecast involved gross oversimplifications. We designed a graphic model - an environmental network - to help us reason through the complexities. An overview of this 3' × 4' graphic model is shown in Fig. 1.

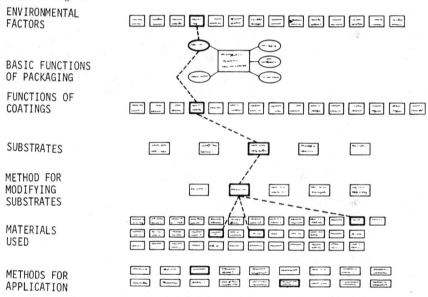

Fig. 1. Pattern of a graphic model relating technical changes in coatings to changes in the environment.

It is impossible to demonstrate adequately this model to a large audience. So let me explain how we identified those areas where changes affecting the future role of coatings in packaging might occur. These identified areas were grouped according to headings on the left-hand side of the figure. Environmental factors include: transportation, changes in marketing and distribution concepts, shifts in the technology of processing products, new package designs, and changes in the forms of products.

The basic functions of packaging include: protection, containment, and stimulation of merchandising and marketing. Coatings protect against grease, water, water vapor, gas, odor; they resist abrasion and scuff, and they can carry print. Substrates include: glass, films and foils, paper and paperboard, rigid and semirigid plastics, and metals. Materials used cover a wide variety of films, foils, polymers, and pigments. Methods of application include reverse roll, transfer roll, gravure, spray, knife and blade, air knife, and many others.

This graphic model was not an end product of the study. It was rather a working tool we used when we were trying to identify changes in the environment and to link them with specific changes in technology. Or, we would use the model when we were trying to identify specific changes in technology that might stimulate changes in the environment. It was a means of reducing "noise" in the system when we were listening for the reply to the question: What should be forecast?

An economist or marketing man, when asked to identify changes in the environment, would report many changes which would have no effect on the coatings themselves. Yet some of his observations would be relevant. Similarly, a technologist would report changes in the technology of polymers, substrates and processes, that would have no effect on coatings. Yet, again, some of his observations would be relevant.

A study that has 'no mechanism for linking relevant changes in the environment with relevant changes in technology contains considerable "noise." Efforts were accordingly directed only along those paths through the network (indicated by the dotted line) where we could define a significant change in the environment and couple it with a significant change in technology. In this way only 20 paths where significant change could be hypothesized were identified.

COMPETING TECHNOLOGIES

This graphic model helped us screen out technical and environmental forces except those which portended significant change in the role of coatings in packaging. But impending change, per se, was insufficient to guide us among competing avenues of technological progress. We examined further the relevant paths. For example, one of these paths starts with "change in the technology of processing products"; e.g., freeze-drying. In order to shed more light on this particular link we developed another graphic model that we have dubbed, an "objectives network." An example of such a network is given in Fig. 2.

This "objectives network" is an example of a technique we evolved for defining strategic business objectives and for translating these objectives into specific technical objectives to guide R & D decision-making. The underlying concept of objectives networking is similar to a number of other techniques that have been reported recently [6, 7, 8]. Time limitations preclude a detailed explanation of the procedures used in structuring the network.

Referring now to Fig. 2, let me indicate briefly how it was constructed. We start with a statement of a strategic objective - in this case, *to exploit the changes in marketing resulting from increased use of freeze-drying for food preservation.* Such an objective might well be a part of a strategic plan of a company in the field of packaging. We

LEVEL I OBJECTIVES -
PACKAGING REQUIRE-
MENTS AND DESIGN

LEVEL II OBJECTIVES -
PROCESSES AND
METHODS

LEVEL III OBJECTIVES -
PERFORMANCE AND
COST

LEVEL IV OBJECTIVES -
DEVELOPMENT ALTER-
NATIVES

LEVEL V OBJECTIVES -
APPLIED RESEARCH
ALTERNATIVES

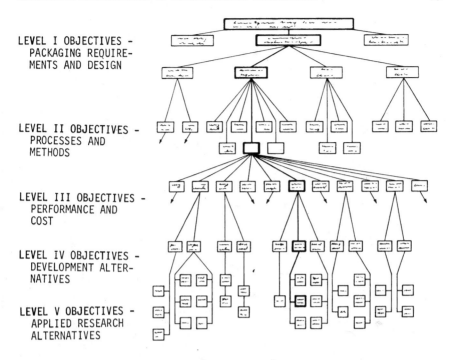

Fig. 2. The pattern of a graphic model: an objectives network

identify a number of sub-objectives that might be pursued by the company
or its competitors. Each sub-objective is then examined to identify sub-
subobjectives. Detailed objectives at Levels III, IV, and V are shown
in Fig. 2 for one sub-objective at Level II. You will note that at each
level there are a number of alternative paths to the preceding level.

Let us now examine a number of the objectives and sub-objectives in
the network.

At the top is a strategic, market-oriented objective: to exploit the
packaging changes required by freeze-dried foods. The next is: to meet
increased requirements for vapor barrier. This, in turn, might be
achieved by one or more of the following:

To develop or use a nonpaper substrate.

To design with a combination of substrate materials

To develop moisture vapor barrier properties on paper substrate

To modify the product, thus reducing need for moisture vapor protection. (I might add that the idea of an edible moisture vapor barrier
might not have occurred to us if we had not been forced to consider alternative objectives in this structured way.)

There is no need to trace through this whole array of structured and
related alternative objectives. It is sufficient to observe that Levels
VI and VII force us to consider alternatives that are at the very frontier
of science.

Before we put this network together most of the detailed alternatives were in the minds of one or another of the Battelle team. In some cases the preparation of the network triggered ideas for new alternatives. The relationships were not at all obvious before the network was structured. Again, I point out that an objectives network is not the end product of an analysis, but simply a working tool. Many empty boxes remain in the network to remind us of alternatives that we have not thought through yet.

Now let us return to the question again: What should be forecast? In relation to Fig. 2, at what level do we need forecasts? What do we want to forecast in detail? What will be directed to the attention of top management? What detail will be of interest to the bench-level researcher? Obviously, for meaningful communications and for purposes of R & D decision-making we want to forecast achievement along competing paths of possible technological progress and at the same time continually search for new paths or new alternatives at any level that might short-cut existing paths.

This array can be restructured by placing at either side the paths that we can reject, *a priori*. In the center we can keep those paths on which we must make more explicit forecasts. By clarifying competing alternatives at every level we can spend as much time or as little as is warranted, using intuitive or formal and sophisticated statistical methods. Where formal statistical methods are practical, relative to the importance of the decision or the degree of risk, they certainly can be used. Their cost can be justified. Data limitations, however, militate against relying on statistical forecasts solely. In other cases, intuitive forecasts are sufficient so long as surveillance is maintained to assure that the initial forecast is correct.

The reason for my concern for the question: *What should be forecast?* is now apparent. Answers to the question limit the options from which valid decisions are possible. They guide in the selection of methods to be used for forecasting. They provide a foundation for communicating the decisions and the logic to both nontechnical executives and to research scientists and engineers. Without this basis for communications the best of forecasts are sterile.

In summary, one of the most serious problems faced by American man management today is rapid technological change. Technological forecasts - explicit and implicit - have been made, are currently being made, and will continue to be made every time a decision is reached regarding R & D or capital budgets. Just to make more explicit the kind of forecasts being made now would be progress. Just to recognize where the rate of technological change has previously been assumed to be k or zero would be helpful. Therefore, improved technological forecasting is urgently needed and such improvement will have a profound impact on industry.

To achieve improvement, however, we must appreciate the hostile environment in which practical technological forecasts must be made and used. To do so means that we place more emphasis on the question: *What should be forecast?*

REFERENCES

1.   KIEFER, David M., Winds of Change in Industrial Chemical Research, *Chemical and Engineering News*, *42*, pp. 88-109, March 23, 1964.

2.   KAY, Hubert, Harnessing the R & D Monster, *Fortune*, *71*:1, pp. 160-3,
     196, 198, January 1965.

3.   GABER, Norman H. and CHEANEY, Edgar S., Taking Some Guesswork Out of
     R & D Investments, *Business Horizons*, 1964.

4.   BRIGHT, James R., *Research Development & Technological Innovation*,
     Homewood, Illinois, Richard D. Irwin, Inc., 1964.

5.   *Proceedings*, Symposium on Decision Theory, Ohio University, October
     3, 1963.

6.   GRANGER, Charles H., The Hierarchy of Objectives, *Harvard Business
     Review*, pp. 63-74, May-June 1964.

7.   MAGEE, John F., Decision Trees for Decision Making, *Harvard Business
     Review*, pp. 126-138, July-August 1964.

8.   KLASS, Philip J., New Approach Pinpoints Vital R & D Needs, *Aviation
     Week & Space Technology*, December 28, 1964, and Rating System Gives
     Planning Priorities, *Aviation Week & Space Technology*, January 4,
     1965.

The preceding essays have emphasized that we can
plan the future of technology, to some extent, by
choosing to allocate resources to certain R & D
efforts, and by choosing not to allocate resources
to other efforts. But what choices are there?
What options are open to us, to accept or reject?
The following essay suggests some of these possibilities, and suggests some of the choices we may
make.

PROSPECTS OF TECHNOLOGICAL PROGRESS*

OLAF HELMER

Institute for the Future, Hartford, Conn., U.S.A.

Much has already been said about the prospects of technological progress during the remainder of this century, and I have little to add to
these prognostications. I would like to use this opportunity, not primarily to make technological forecasts, but to discuss the role that the
forecasting of technological developments plays in shaping the future
of our society. In presenting some specific forecasts for the year
2000, I would like merely to provide a certain amount of substantive
illustrative material for such a discussion.

The year 2000, with which this conference is concerned, is only one
third of a century away from us. But the pace of change in our time,
due to scientific and technological advances, is greater than it used
to be and is still accelerating. Consequently, the world of 2000 will
be far less like our present world than our present world is like that
of a third of a century ago. Thus a high degree of uncertainty has to be
attached to many things we may wish to say about the year 2000.

Nevertheless, quite a few statements can be made with some confidence about the world of the future. Let me give a few examples.

It is virtually certain that:

The world population will be over 5 billion.

The rate of population increase will have begun to decelerate, due
to the widespread acceptance of cheap and effective means of fertility
control.

Absolute food production will be substantially higher that it is
today, aided primarily by large-scale desalination of sea water.

The world GNP will be more than 3 times and possibly 4 times what
it is today, resulting probably in an approximate doubling and possibly
in a tripling of per-capita GNP.

People will largely live in urban complexes, surrounded by numerous
automata. In particular, there will be central data banks and libraries
with fully automated access, a credit card economy in which cash trans-
actions will be virtually eliminated, highly sophisticated teaching machines will be in wide use, portable video telephones will facilitate

---

*This paper was prepared for presentation at a conference of the
Japan Economic Research Council in Tokyo in September 1967.

communication among persons everywhere, and this process will be further
enhanced by the availability of automated translation from one language
to another.

Personality-affecting drugs will be as widely used and accepted as
alcoholic beverages are today.

The life span of many people will be extended through the common
practice of replacing worn or diseased organs by implanting artificial
plastic and electronic organs.

A permanent colony will exist on the Moon, and men will almost certainly have landed on Mars.

Not quite so certain as the statements just made, but still very
probable, are the following:

Controlled thermonuclear power will be economically competitive
with other sources of power.

It will be possible to control the weather regionally to a large
extent.

Ocean mining on a large scale will be in progress.

Artificial life will have been created in the test tube.

Immunization against all bacterial and viral diseases will be available.

Highly intelligent machines will exist that will act as effective
collaborators of scientists and engineers.

Next let me list a few developments that are less probable but
still have a good chance of being part of the world of 2000:

Large-scale ocean farming may be practiced.

Our highway transportation may be fully automated.

Cooperation between man and machine may have progressed to the point
of actual symbiosis, in the sense of enabling man to extend his intelligence by direct electromechanical interaction between his brain and a
computing machine.

We may have learned, through molecular engineering, to control here-
ditary defects in man, to control the aging process, and to induce the
artificial growth of new limbs and organs. We may also have drugs available that raise a person's level of intelligence.

In space, we may be mining ores and manufacturing propellents on
the Moon, we may have established a permanent Mars base, and we may have
landed on Jupiter's moons.

This sample of forecasts, I think, will provide a sufficient substantive background for the following discussion, which will be focus-
sing upon three considerations: (i) the changed role that forecasts
play in our thinking about the future of our society, (ii) some of the
specific tasks that lie ahead in organizing a systematic analysis of
the future, and (iii) the prospects of accomplishing these tasks in
the decades before us.

The purpose of long-range forecasts generally is not just to satisfy mankind's persistent curiosity about its future destiny, but the main
objective of such forecasts is to inform decision-makers in both the public and private sectors of a nation of potential future dangers that must

be avoided and of potential future opportunities that must be seized.

This new, pragmatic, view of the value of forecasting is of relatively recent origin. It reflects a wholly new attitude toward the future among planners and researchers. The fatalistic view of the future as unforeseeable but unique and hence inevitable has been abandoned. We see instead a growing awareness that there is a whole spectrum of possible futures, with varying degrees of probability, and that through proper planning we may exert considerable influence over these probabilities. Although our control over the future, which we might thus aspire to exercise, is merely marginal, we have learned from the economists that small marginal adjustments in planning the domestic affairs of a nation can make all the difference between misery and contentedness for large segments of its people.

This newly acquired realization of our power to affect our own destiny through deliberate long-range planning brings with it a new social responsibility for the scientist and analyst. It falls upon him to provide the kind of comprehensive analysis of the future on which the political process of influencing the future must rest.

A responsible analysis of the future calls for a program with these three components:

1. *A survey of alternatives,* that is, a full exploration of potential future developments, together with estimates of their *a priori* probabilities; and a description of the major alternatives with regard to the future state of the world in terms of coherent conglomerations of such developments.

2. *An analysis of preferences,* that is, an explication of the extent to which the pursuit of any particular alternative state would serve the public interest. In this context, "the public interest" may well have to be viewed from several standpoints, namely, as seen by the executive branch of its government, and - in some sense - as seen by the world community. This analysis of differential preferences should in no way prejudge the issues. Rather, by analyzing the moral implications of professed attitudes and the degree to which the probable consequences of contemplated policies would comply with them, it should enhance the rationality of the democratic decision-making process.

3. *Constructive policy research:* Having aided the process of selecting the more desirable among the possible futures of the world, the final and most demanding step is that of devising the means of attaining these futures, or at least of raising their probabilities of occurrence as much as possible through appropriate policies and programs.

These then, summed up briefly, are the obvious desiderata: To find out about the possible futures that lie ahead; to single out the more desirable ones among them; and to invent the instrumentalities for their deliberate pursuit.

An organized effort to enhance our capability, as analysts, to deal with these three tasks is prerequisite to putting the process of shaping the future of our society on a more rational foundation. It constitutes the basis for the application of social technology, that is, for the invention of social institutions and the design of social policies that promise to fulfill our reasonable aspirations. And it is on the prospects of socio-technological progress, in this sense, that I want to concentrate in the remainder of this paper.

The prospects of substantial socio-technological progress during the third third of this century, in my opinion, are very high. I base this optimism on four clearly recognizable trends.

One is the ongoing, explosively increasing, effort devoted to scientific research generally. Judging by the trend during the second third of the century and extrapolating very conservatively, the world's scientific manpower in the year 2000 is likely to be at least five times what it is today. In addition, because of the availability of more sophisticated instruments and, above all, of more powerful computing machines, the productivity of the individual researcher is apt to rise at the very least by a factor of two. Consequently we may expect the total rate of scientific productivity to grow at least tenfold by the end of the century. The increased understanding of the world we live in that is implied by this development is the first reason for my optimism regarding socio-technological progress.

The second reason, already partly implied by the first, is the second computer revolution, which is already well under way. It took just twenty years for the first computer revolution to be completed, from the mid-forties to the mid-sixties, during which time the computer grew up from being a bookkeeping device to becoming a highly versatile data processor and research tool. During that period the size and the cost of electronic computer components have gone down by factors of 100 and 100,000 respectively, and their speed has gone up by a factor of 100,000.

While these trends will continue for some time and, together with long-distance time-sharing arrangements, will account during the next decade for a continued annual doubling of the amount of computer power in the world, the second computer revolution will add a significantly new flavor to this resource of ours. It will consist of the amalgamation of two separate trends, which in combination promise to have a powerful impact on planning processes generally. They are (i) the relative automation of the computer, in the sense of doing away with many of the cumbersome aspects of computer programming and thereby facilitating direct communication between the individual researcher and the computer; and (ii) the invention of numerous highly versatile display devices, coupled directly to the computer, that permit a designer to construct visual and, when necessary, moving images of his ideas as he develops them. These two trends, which are well under way, will constitute the beginning of a true symbiosis between man and machine, where in a very real sense man's intelligence will be enhanced through collaboration with a computer.

My third reason for taking a bright view of future progress in social technology is that there is yet another, subtle, revolution in the making, namely a reorientation among social scientists toward policy-related research. Instead of continuing the relatively futile endeavor to emulate the physical *sciences*, researchers in the social-science area are realizing that the time has come to emulate physical *technology*. They are beginning to do this by seeking an interdisciplinary systems approach to the solution of socio-political problems. They will accomplish this by transferring the methods of operations research from the area of physical technology to that of social technology.

The potential reward from this evolving reorientation of some of the effort in the social-science area toward social technology, employing operations-analytical techniques, is considerable; it may even equal or exceed in importance that of the achievements credited to the technologies arising out of the physical sciences.

Operations analysis was first brought into being through the
exigencies of World War II; it has since continued to develop and become
a widely accepted tool, not only in the peacetime management of military
affairs, but throughout the operations commerce and industry.

Among the principal operations research techniques that have proven
themselves in these areas and that show great promise of being transfer-
able to that of social technology are the construction of mathematical
models, simulation procedures, and a systematic approach to the utilization of intuitive expert judgment. All of these techniques - it is
almost needless to say - are greatly aided and continually refined through
the availability of the computer, and the second computer revolution
which I described may well add another order of magnitude to their potency.
In particular, automated access to central data banks, in conjunction with
appropriate socioeconomic models, will provide the soft sciences with the
same kind of massive data processing and interpreting capability that,
in the physical sciences, created the breakthrough which led to the understanding and management of atomic energy.

One of the results of the greater receptivity of social scientists
to mathematical models and to an interdisciplinary systems approach may
well be the development of a comprehensive theory of organizations, where
by this term I mean the general discipline concerned with human interactions in decision-making situations. Taken in this sense, organization
theory is a direct extension of the so-called theory of games, - an extension which it is necessary to achieve before we can deal with social conflict situations that the present theory has been unable to resolve. Any
form of social interaction, be it among persons or among business firms
or among states, can be viewed as a game we are playing, or rather a continuing series of games, in which in some sense we strive to maximize our
individual or corporate or national utilities. The next great breakthrough in the social sciences, comparable in significance to such physical breakthroughs as the creation of artificial life or the control of
thermonuclear energy, may well be the construction of a theory of organizations that succeeds in dealing rationally with situations of inter-
personal or international conflict. My expectation that this breakthrough will occur is my fourth reason for hope in this general area.

How, specifically, will all these developments lead to improvements
in the analysis of the future? How, in de Jouvenel's phrase, will they
advance the "art of conjecture"?

I described earlier the three parts of which an analysis of the
future has to consist. Let us reexamine them briefly.

The survey of possible futures, with which any analysis of the future
must begin, will continue to have to rely primarily on the intuitive judgment of experts. The process of obtaining a consensus among specialists
will be enormously improved through the developments which I mentioned.
Not only will the expected gigantic increase in scientific knowledge
raise the quality of available expertise by an order or magnitude, but
the day is not too far off when we can establish a world-wide network of
specialists, each equipped with a console tied to one central computer
and to electronic data banks, who will be able to interact with one
another via the computer network and thus obtain a consensus among themselves through a process of which the present-day Delphi technique is a
primitive precursor. Aside from procedural refinements in this technique, one of the major improvements that will have to be introduced is
that potential future developments will not be inquired into in isolation
but that proper attention will be paid to cross-correlations among such

developments. For instance, the occurrence of one development may raise the probability of occurrence of another either because it facilitates the other technologically or because it makes the other socially more desirable. A systematic treatment of such cross-influences will be a necessary ingredient of any future survey of possible futures.

With regard to the analysis of preferences, which is the second component of an analysis of the future, I expect that the general reorientation of the social sciences toward policy-directed systems research will lead to considerable advances in the selection and measurement of social indicators. Organization theory, in particular, if it develops in the direction which I outlined, will permit us to view a nation as an organization of individuals, or the world as an organization of nations, in which the members have partly conflicting goals. We may then be able to attack the problem of the welfare of such communities more rationally by dealing with it within the systematic framework of a theory of organizational preferences.

Finally, there is the third aspect of the art of conjecture, namely the matter of constructive policy research. Here we are in the area of what may be called the systematization of social inventiveness. *It* is apt to benefit most profoundly from the acceptance of operations-research techniques within the social sciences. Program-budgeting, especially, will come of age, by utilizing the conceptual framework of organizational utilities and preferences that we may expect organization theory to furnish. Comprehensive simulated planning by multidisciplinary groups of experts, aided by electronic computers and display devices as well as by sophisticated mathematical models, will result in alternative developmental scenarios. Judging by past experience, the stimulating effect of interacting within a simulated environment will be highly conducive to inventiveness and imagination among the participants, and we may well look forward to the emergence of a new breed of modern-day constructive utopians, who will invent not only better futures but the social instrumentalities of attaining them.

In summary then, in view of what may reasonably be expected, the potential progress of social technology that lies within the grasp of the next generation is tremendous. First these new methods will find their application within the societies of the advanced nations. But the pace of events is fast in this century, and before it is over I think there is hope that international relations will not remain unaffected by such progress, so that some of us may live to see the beginning of the era when the ample resources of the world will be equitably distributed among all nations, and war will be obsolescent.

The preceding essay discussed some
of the things the future may have
in store for us. A great many technological advances will be found
entirely feasible. Must we accept
them, simply because of their feasibility? Does the fact that they are
possible mean that they are inevitable? In the following essay, Dr.
Ozbekhan examines this question.

THE TRIUMPH OF TECHNOLOGY: "CAN IMPLIES OUGHT"*

HASAN OZBEKHAN

King Resources Co., Los Angeles, Calif., U.S.A.

I.

The theme of this paper, which is really part of a larger general
subject that might be called "The Quality of Life in the Future," will be
discussed in terms of normative planning. Without dwelling on prelimi-
naries, during which definitions would need to be established, assumptions
ordered, and clarifications - semantic as well as logical - provided so
that the argument following can be glued together as tightly and neatly
as possible, this discussion will move directly to the somewhat special
perspective of "planning." Such a perspective may help to organize a
number of surrounding points into a pattern, in ways that are not always
obvious and in terms of a frame of relationships that may lead to some
interesting conjectures.

II.

The title "The Triumph of Technology: "'Can' implies 'Ought,'" is
almost a riddle, to be approached with some degree of indirection. Otherwise its meaning may be hard to uncover. Yet this difficulty of approach
does afford some freedom.

The title describes a special conjuncture created by "technology,"
"can," and "ought." The situation underlying this conjuncture is one in
which we view technology as triumphant. It is with this situation that
we will begin.

There are, no doubt, many ways of judging what the advent of the technological age has done to—as well as for—mankind. It has changed and is
changing, under our very eyes, the face of the physical environment both in
the technologically advanced and the technologically backward countries, although the advanced countries are more visibly affected by the direct application of science and engineering to the environment. Probably more important by far is what the age of technology has done to the geography of human
outlook and expectation. In this area it would be wrong to make assessments
that differentiate between countries and peoples, as here the effects of
technology are universal and by their very nature represent a unifying force.

* This material originally appeared in Planning for Diversity and Choice,
edited by Stanford Anderson, and is used with the permission of the copyright
holder, MIT Press.

They could perhaps be described as having led to a generalized phenomenon
of expansion: of possibilities, knowledge, ambition, mobility, relationships, needs, wants. All this is not so much an external happening as it
is an experience, an event of the mind. Nevertheless, the event is occurring throughout the world, affecting, in various ways but strongly,
the American, the European, the Asian, the African – whoever and wherever
he may be.

Events of this magnitude have a price. The price of this particular
event is that sense of strange and powerful disquiet we feel in the face
of the heaving horizon that confronts us. Old institutions, known ways
of life, established relations, defined functions, well-traced frontiers
of knowledge and feeling – all are changing as we go. We are constantly
subjected to new configurations of perceived reality; we are constantly
asked to adapt faster and faster to requirements generated by new information, by a narrowing and always changing physical environment, by an
increasingly confused and proliferating set of goals, outlooks, and aspirations. It is as though the entire environment of man – all the dimensions of his ecological, social, political, emotional, and physical
space – were becoming less solid, less permanent, and less constant. It
would seem as though we were in the midst of a vast process of *ephemeral-
ization* or *liquefaction*.

Within this process, interlinked with it, and activated by it, the
old problems remain, or renew themselves, Phoenix-like: famine in India,
upheavals in China, lack of industrialization in all underdeveloped
countries, a confused and confusing revival of nationalism in Europe,
warring ideologies and interests in Vietnam, relative deepening of poverty among the poor, relative growth of despair among the young – the
multiple disequilibria of a world in full expansion and constant flux
in which expectations and achievements fail to match.

To repeat, there are no doubt different judgments that one can pass
on such a situation. However, the passing of a judgment is fruitful only
insofar as it leads to decision and action. Yet, in the case of the
larger dynamics of our situation, it would appear that there is not much
we can do any longer – it is all, by now, probably beyond our control.
As Pascal said, "You are embarked" – and, once we are embarked, "*Il faut
parier*" – we have to wager. There is no choice. What counts are the
ends we shall put our bets on.

                                    III.

But these ends, these *goals* as we would rather may in our epoch,
what are they? How are they revealed, implemented, attained? To answer
these questions, we must look more closely at the situation, at how we
came to it and at what we brought into it.

When our situation is viewed in its current immediacy its most
striking aspect is complexity. When we try to imagine it in terms of the
future what strikes us most are the uncertainties it unfolds in the mind.
Thus we stand, perhaps more conscious and knowing than ever before, in
the grip of present worldwide complexities and future uncertainties trying
to define those modes of action that will best order the one and reduce
the other.

The organizing principles of these modes of action are what we have
recently become reconciled, with some reluctance, to calling "planning."

The notion of planning did not come easily, because we did not arrive in total innocence at this pass in our affairs. We reached it armed with traditions, institutions, philosophies, self-images, achievements, failures, hypocrisies, prejudices, languages, values, and a world view: in other words, with everything that ultimately adds up to that state of mind called Western Civilization - with a capital W and a capital C.

Western Civilization, the ground and essence of technological civilization, is however, the very complicated result of very complicated forces that were set in motion partly during the Renaissance by Galileo and partly during the eighteenth century - the Age of Enlightenment. Like other civilizations, ours is (or used to be) a way of life in which uncertainty is reduced by means of stable and dependable continuities while complexity is organized into those routines we call institutions.

During its long history, however, Western Civilization also developed certain characteristic features, with regard to freedom and the individual's decision-making role, that permitted it to accomodate a great deal of loosely controlled initiative and even of venturesomeness. In fact, it could be said that our civilization nurtured two of its contrary inner tendencies with astonishing care and insistence: One was a deep commitment to detailed molecular disorder, which it cherished as the stepchild of liberty; the other was an almost superstitious belief in the idea of automatism (as exemplified by Adam Smith's "hidden hand," or by the extraordinary notion of laissez-faire equilibrium), which it viewed as capable of regulating the disorder into a livable environment. This commitment to microcosmic disorder and concomitant trust in the automatism of macroprocesses - including social processes - are, in some truly nontrivial ways, the progenitors of our present situation.

Planning, in the sense we are beginning to understand it - as informed decision and calculated action - refutes and rejects both these parents. That is why we came to it late and with reluctance; that is why we are still half-hearted about it. Clearly, we are not yet convinced that a reduction in social or political randomness need not necessarily result in a grievous narrowing of acquired freedoms; and although we have learned at great cost (the last major settling of accounts and paying of bills being the Great Depression) that what we took to be automatism in social processes was nothing but a myth, we are still not wholly reconciled to the proposition that conscious and rational decision making at the sources of power might be effective in reducing the uncertainties of the future.

Of our two basic tendencies, the long-run effects of automatism have undoubtedly been the more disastrous insofar as the current state of planning is concerned, for the cast of mind that was able to rationalize automatism into a jealously protected belief was also the cast of mind that, almost unconsciously, shaped our initial conception of planning.

This initial conception was formulated when it seemed natural to be inspired for our basic planning model by one of the enduring and no doubt fruitful traits of classical Western thought, which is a pragmatic commitment to determinism in various forms. The deterministic model of planning is both simple and elegant. It tells us that there is sequentiality and linearity in events and that what we call the "future" descends in direct line from the past and can be explained in the same way. The fundamental tool of deterministic planning is extrapolation. The fundamental result of extrapolation is a single outcome, or future. In

such a model the decision variables yield a single future for each decision. Among such parallel futures, issued from parallel decisions, one
can then choose in accordance with a preestablished system of values.
Some outcomes are good, while some are bad, if one knows what good and
bad are. Consequently, one plans in terms of the decision that is going
to yield the good, or at any rate the best possible outcome. Thus, some
futures are more advantageous than others, less painful than others, some
more worthwhile than the rest combined. The choice is always clear as
long as the value system that serves as frame of reference remains solidly and operationally grounded, and as long as there are institutions to
enforce it within a particular environment.

The great weaknesses of deterministic planning are obvious: First,
there is the inability to accept events that are exogenous to the single
closed decision system that is its main constituent. Second, and, as we
are only now discovering, by far its most crippling feature, is that it
postulates and requires a value system that is given and constant and
outside both the conceptual boundaries and the operational jurisdiction
of the planning process. Clearly, the choices such planning offers could
never be concerned with ethical alternatives that find expression in
"oughts"; they are concerned instead with feasibility - "can" it be done?
- namely, with technoeconomic alternatives.

Since the end of the Second World War, the economic component of the
technoeconomic equation has weakened considerably. Abundance, relative
though it may be, has lifted a great many of the limitations that scarcity
had imposed on the spectrum of open choices. With this, technological
feasibility has tended increasingly to become the sole criterion of decisions and action. Thus, technology, as many in recent years have pro-
claimed with increasing shrillness, has grown into the central, all-per-
vasive, governing experience of Western man today.

One of the results of this encroachment has been that we are now
envisioning our future almost exclusively in relation to alternatives
predicated on feasibility, or "can." And because the realm of what we
actually can do has expanded almost beyond belief, feasibility tends to
define our ends and to suggest the only goals we are willing to entertain.
"Can" has almost unconsciously and insidiously begun to imply, and therefore replace, "ought."

This evolution has been strengthened and encouraged by the neglect
into which, since the eighteenth century, our traditional values or
"oughts" have fallen. The confines to vision and action imposed by these
"oughts" have been pierced here, overcome there, obliterated in most
places. We continuously failed to develop a new ethic commensurate with
our technology, yet the old ethic lost much of its meaning and guiding
power. It has become abstract - hence operationally invalid as a policy-
making or planning tool.

Today, in the situation that surrounds us, to act in the light of
old dicta that used to relate the "good" to events - e.g., population increase is good, or the extension of the benefits of modern medicine to
all men is good, or individual high productivity and hard work and thrift
are good, or education for everybody is good - means to act blindly and
to contribute to a set of vast consequences whose risks or even value
content (namely, whose goodness) we have no way of calculating or judging.
None of the above instances may be bad, but we can no longer be unques-
tioningly certain that they are good.

Having made these points, let us now attempt to clarify what the
title of this paper really means in planning terms. It means that in a
technology-dominated age such as ours, and as a result of forces that
have brought this dominance about, "can," a conditional and neutral expression of feasibility, begins to be read as if it were written "ought,"
which is an ethical statement connoting an imperative. Thus, feasibility,
which is a strategic concept, becomes elevated into a normative concept,
with the result that whatever technological reality indicates we *can* do
is taken as implying that we *must* do it. The strategy dictates its own
goal. The action defines its own telos. Aims no longer guide invention;
inventions reveal aims. Or, in McLuhan's now fashionable slogan, "The
medium is the message."

In sum, the above-mentioned developments have had two major effects
on the deterministic planning model outlined earlier: First, the power
and scope of strategies open to us have been increased and enlarged to
the point where it is no longer possible to make sense of any method that
derives a single outcome from a given decision. Second, the model has
lost the independent frame of values that once made it operative. It has
not only lost it, it has taken it over, swallowed it, ingested it. In
spite of this, we have not developed a new operational model. Hence, we
are no longer sure of the direction in which our momentum is taking us.

The recognition of this fact is the source of the general disquiet
most of us seem to share. And this disquiet can, probably, be reduced to
the following question: Is feasibility a good enough end to pursue, and
by which to reach decisions and calculate human risks and consequences of
action in these perilous and complex time?

Offhand, the answer seems to be "No." But this "No" needs to be
probed, elaborated, and operationally understood; and, if possible, some
positive solutions need to be pointed out. Let us try to do this with
reference to some emerging conceptions in planning theory, policy, and
implementation.

IV.

Today, in many countries, including those of capitalist persuasion,
something called "planning" is going on. In fact, it appears possible
now to ascribe much of the unexpected success of Western economics to the
systematic application of this particular type of economic calculus at
the government level. Generally speaking, the attitudes that underlie
this application have been derived from welfare economics while most of
the operational concepts and tools that have been adopted are Keynesian
in origin.

All this activity, which involves great effort, is still relatively
primitive. It is built on a number of desirables such as government control of extreme fluctuations, international balances, investment trends,
employment, etc. More recently, attempts have been made to extend it to
social fields such as housing, urban development, education, health, old
age, and poverty. For the moment, the results of these newer attempts do
not appear too impressive. There is a sense of floundering - a feeling
that we don't exactly know where it is we want to end up, or that we have
not really understood the problems we are trying to solve. The words
that have guided us along our paths are a set of reasoned cliches: Some
still talk in terms of Keynes' particular vision of the "civilized life,"
others prefer to stand by something they call the "dignity of man," still

others find inspiration in the "fulfillment of the human being." In the
United States we have even derived a number of National Goals from similar desirables that have since been costed-out and priority-ordered in
relation to expected economic growth through 1975.

Our approach to all this has been unimpeachably orthdox: From inbred
notions of the good we have derived a selected number of socioeconomic
desirables and translated them into a set of socioeconomic problems. The
criterion for translation was the feasible, and the calculus of the feasible was mostly economic in character. So now we know that, if the GNP
grows as forecast, by 1975 we shall be able to do certain things. From
this point we generally pass to the implementation phase.

What we have failed to do in all this is to ascribe operational
meaning to the so-called desirables that motivate us, to question their
intrinsic worth, to assess the long-range consequences of our aspirations
and actions, to wonder whether the outcome we seem to be expecting does
in fact correspond to that *quality of life* we say we are striving for -
and whether our current actions will lead us there. In other words, in
this writer's conception of planning we are in the deeper sense failing
to plan.

One of the major causes of our failure to plan is that, the human
mind being what it is, it would appear almost impossible to plan without
a conceptual and philosophical framework made up of integrative principles - in short, without a generally accepted theory of planning. We
have not succeeded yet in developing such a theory.

Whenever this point is raised, the difficulties that surround such
an undertaking (and that also explains its lack) become crystal clear,
and the questions grow tense. In such a theory is one to deal with facts
or goals? With the present or future? Are we concerned with continuity
or new departures? Should one write for planners or policy makers? And
so on.

These very questions indicate how much our intellectual traditions
stand in the way of the needs we feel, how much our positivist inheritance
vitiates our ability to grapple with the normative requirements of policy
generation. Yet, despite such obstacles, the foundations for a unifying
theory of planning must be laid. Hence, an effort will be made here to
answer the above questions.

Much of what has been said up to this point shows this writer's personal conception of planning to consist of three interrelated approaches
that could be formulated as three plans that unfold in conjunction with
each other. These are: the normative plan, which deals with "oughts" and
defines the goals on which all policy rests; the strategic plan, which
formulates what, in the light of elected "oughts," or chosen policies, we
can actually do; and, finally, the operational plan, which establishes
how, when, and in what sequence of action we *will* implement the strategies
that have been accepted as capable of satisfying the policies. Thus, a
planning-relevant framework needs, in this particular conception, always
to reveal what *ought* to be done, what *can* be done, and what actually *will*
be done.

Strategic and operational planning fit more or less well into current practice. Normative planning, however, is not seriously considered
yet as an integral element of that same practice. Policy considerations
still remain outside the planning process and enter into it as exogenous

givens. In the system outlined above, such a differentiation would not exist. Policy making, strategy definition, and the determination of implementing steps would be viewed as parts of a single, integrated, iterative process.

Normative planning has interesting conceptual dimensions that should be noted briefly. To begin with, it deals with the consequences of value dynamics, hence with the delineation of qualitative futures. In this sense, it abolishes the old distinction between goals and facts in favor of viewing goals *as* facts, thereby ascribing to them the necessary practical weights. Similarly, it is in the course of normative planning that some new approaches to temporal relationships and interactions between what we call the present and the future are recognized and established. To use a play on words, we might say that the future is the *subject* of normative planning, but the present is its *object*. A close analysis of the consequences of value dynamics reveals not just one *single* future deducible from the parameters of a given decision but a multiplicity of discrete possible futures that have to be delineated and explored. Any choice, under these circumstances, tends to apply to a spectrum of states, thus enlarging the entire field of decisions. And, again, decisions made in the light of such future "images" initiate that backward chain of calculable events that, once they reach the present, can be translated into it in the form of calculated "change." The possibility of acting upon present reality by starting from an imagined or anticipated future situation affords great freedom to the decision maker while at the same time providing him with better controls with which to guide events. Thus, planning becomes in the true sense "futures-creative" and the very fact of anticipating becomes causative of action. It is at this point that the policy maker-planner is able to free himself from what René Dubos has called the "logical future," and operate in the light of a "willed future."

It is the introduction of this element of conscious and informed will into the system that frees us from the remnants of automatism while at the same time allowing real policy considerations directly to enter the planning process.

It would be a mistake to believe that this method represents some rather convoluted way of making long-range predictions. On the contrary, the actual assertion is that planning does not really *deal* with the future as we think of it – it deals with the present, inasmuch as it concerns itself with possible consequences that action taken in the face of future uncertainties will have on the present. Planning is directed toward the future not so that one can predict what is there, for clearly there *is* nothing *there*. (The forecasts we make about things like population increase, resource availability, etc., are obviously not based on what is there, but on what was here in the past, what is here in the present, and what we *think* the configurations of these things will be some years hence.) Planning is directed to the future to "invent" it (as Denis Gabor has said) or to "construct" it (as Pierre Massé has put it). And this is done to reduce uncertainties that confront current decisions by encapsulating each decision within a firm enough normative "image" to provide the kind of information needed to attain the desired ends.

The fundamental questions with which normative planning must be approached are: If this good/ then what future situation? If that situation/ then is it good? What this amounts to is saying: If we want full employment, education, health, housing, equality, etc., we must want them for certain calculable reasons that will be reflected in a new situation.

Hence, we must determine: full employment for what? Education for what?
Health for what? Housing for what? Equality for what? Only as a result
of such determinations can we define which possible outcome will really
correspond to what today we keep calling "the civilized life," "fulfil-
ment of the human being," and "the dignity of man." If we don't plan in
this manner, then we in fact may continue to act in good faith but without
knowing whether our actions can satisfy the ends we have in mind. Nor
will we obtain enough alternative solutions to achieve some workable (op-
timizing) conjunction. The latter point is important because one of our
problems consists in the requirement that we achieve several such goals
simultaneously; we are no longer advancing step by step.

Perhaps the major lesson to be derived from these very sketchy considerations is that in normative planning the important thing is not to
be surpassed or overcome by current events. This always tends to happen.
Whenever it does happen, planning reverts to becoming mainly responsive
to current situations rather than creative of future, and as long as planning is not futures-creative, it must be an after-the-fact ordering exercise dominated by present events. Such an exercise is, obviously, not
planning, but something less.

Now let us discuss briefly the next phase of the planning effort -
strategic planning. As has been repeatedly noted, strategic planning is
grounded in the concept of feasibility. However, if feasibility is approached as a parameter rather than as a norm, then its nature changes.
The major result of establishing norms and assessing feasibility in their
light is the effect of freeing policy making from its traditional prison
of "expediency" and beginning to understand it in terms of "relevance."
Expediency is often confused with practicality, which is undoubtedly important, but, in terms of the line of thought developed in this paper, it
is clear that a multiplicity of goals based on a multiplicity of norms
enlarges the traditional boundaries of the practical and thereby broadens
the spectrum of alternative policies among which we are called to choose.
Thus, in strategic planning, that which can be done must always refer to
a particular number of alternatives that have grown from work done in the
normative stage. There is no doubt a narrowing of vision at this point,
but this narrowing is a result of the elimination of conflicting alternative possibilities that, under the circumstances, have been found either
irrelevant or insoluble. What is eliminated is the open-ended perspective, which, while deepening perception, paralyses action. What is introduced is coherence, numbers, milestones, steps, intermediate or in-
process configurations that are relevant to the ends we have chosen. It
is during this phase that one of the most difficult aspects of planning
is encountered. It consists in formulating objective action links between
the norm, or the "ought," and the "can." It is at this point that the
analysis is made of whether or not a particular goal is relevant to a
particular situation and to a particular strategy. Here again, the issue
is not so much whether the earlier parts of the plan are feasible as
whether or not they are consonant with reality and whether such a conson-
ance can be translated into the probable realization of the goals themselves. The issue to emphasize in this progression is that solutions to
subsystemic problems are approached not with reference to the subsystem
itself, but to a predetermined meta-system that permits the encompassing
and the ordering of the alternative strategies that such solutions define.

Now, finally, the last step, operational planning, is reached. This
consists mainly in the determination of how to implement the adopted
strategies. In some sense, it is the phase of the plan that delineates
what *will* be done. It is during this phase that a translation takes

place from the plausible to the probable. The set of priority-ordered interlooking decisions, of course, must foresee, within the temporal framework, a continuity of action, and, in its turn, that continuity of action must be so conceived as to be able to overcome the momentary uncertainties, the immediate disjunctions that every act creates, if, as it must, it creates change within a given system.

Taken together, the general outline of the planning methodology developed in the preceding pages constitutes a continuum – a self-feeding application of intellective analysis and synthesis to events, whereby the present processes of society and of organization can be constantly guided with reference to the future. It is in this sense that we must understand planning as representing a fundamental and uninterrupted activity, whether it takes place in the corporation, the city, the nation, international relations, or whatever it is we choose to call "environment."

Of the three phases of planning just described, we know more (in empirical terms) about strategic planning and operational planning than we know about normative planning. For the first two, we have borrowed from certain commonly used methodologies, which will therefore be merely mentioned here – such things as systems analysis, system design, operations research, simulation, etc. The introduction of the computer into our lives and the advances we are making in natural language processing – an advance that will permit nonprogrammers to deal directly with the computer – has greater enlarged our ability to question a wide variety of facts and variables. Our main effort should therefore be directed to the development of methodologies and techniques having the same kind of power for the making of normative plans. In this area we are lagging. And in this area the point is not, as it is often purported to be, that we should make efforts to eliminate man and computerize the entire system, but rather that we should develop a greater understanding of how to relate the computer to man in more efficient ways so that we can benefit from technology in our attempts to firm up a theory of normative planning.

V.

Earlier in this paper it was stated that what counted were the ends we put our bets on. That statement obviously leads to the question: What are the possible ends – if feasibility, by itself, is insufficient? In this concluding section, let us review the portions of the present analysis that may contain clues concerning an answer to that question.

To begin with, it seems obvious that the goals of practical human action cannot be established as immutable truths, and that each situation encompasses a conjuncture that, if anticipated, operationally defined, and caused to happen might satisfy whatever is generally considered as good in a particular civilization at a particular time. The problem, therefore, is not in reinventing the good, but in being able to redefine it in terms of meanings that have the most value for us, in our present state. The dynamics of our situation is such that we can no longer be sure of being able, automatically, to derive *consequences* we *can* judge as good from *actions* we *do* judge as good. Somehow the ability to link the value of a present act to the value of its chosen consequences must be created and made operational. Only such a link will permit us to determine those ends we should be betting on.

An attempt has been made here to outline the idea of such a link in terms of a particular planning approach. In the formulation given, goal

valuation is integrated into the planning process itself. For this manner of planning we lack two things: first, a worked-out theory and methodology; second, the required institutional setting. These, clearly, are
very major shortcomings.

Insofar as theory and methodology are concerned, it is evident that
our current economic calculus is not enough. We need something in the
nature of a social accounting system as well as a value calculus (an
axiology) to supplement it. Some work is being done in both these areas
but it is as yet at a very tentative stage. Insofar as the institutional
setting is concerned, progress is very slow--a fact that needs no elabor-
ation here.

In this connection, it should nevertheless be noted that a still
ill-defined symbiosis, or at least a symbiotic interaction, between technique, theory, and institutional setting appears to exist. The absence
of theory inhibits our ability to extend our techniques to the field of
norm definition and goal valuation. Theory building, in turn, is affected by our current institutions. This is visible mainly in the difficulty
we experience in determining *who* is going to plan. This difficulty arises
partly from our political tradition, which often views solutions that satisfy individual self-interest as the major expression of freedom in
society. This tends to make us look upon any extensive planning--namely,
system-wide integrated solutions--with grave misgivings, as being outside
the mainstream of the concepts that underlie our political organization.
This, of course, is frustrating, for it is indeed difficult to see how any
alteration in our planning can be obtained without ultimately raising some
basic questions about our current institutional arrangements. We do not
know whether the answer to this dilemma lies in pluralistic, or advocate,
or expert planning.

We do know, however, that the power of ideas is very great. What
Keynes used to call the "primitive stage" of the argument is probably
behind us. After this stage, many things become possible. There is
some ground now on which we can stand. The European experiment in planning is a prodding example for us. In the United States we have, after
all, concluded that massive unemployment ought not to be allowed. We
have decided that economic fluctuations are onerous and that they ought
to be controlled. We have committed ourselves to certain notions of
equality with regard to the distribution of wealth, with regard to education, with regard to civil rights, even though we have not been too
successful in defining the "what for" of these commitments beyond the
words "The Great Society". In short, we seem to have understood that
these "oughts" will not occur by themselves, that there is no automatism in social processes that transcends human will and calculated
action. We should now be able to exert that will in developing the
knowledge and information that will sustain it. Only by that means
can we succeed in distinguishing the real problems from the false ones,
and choosing among real answers--that is, answers that have some degree
of precision, and are capable of showing us some direction in this
present of ours which contains all the future we can ever hope to
have.

In the following essay, Mr. Goldsen
stresses the point that the future
is man-made. We can have the future we choose to have, and forecasting is useful in telling us
what are the futures we can choose
among.

THINKING ABOUT FUTURE SOCIAL DEVELOPMENT

JOSEPH M. GOLDSEN

*Concilium on International and Area Studies, Yale University,
New Haven, Conn., U.S.A.*

Your theme for this morning is "What Can We Expect? - Prospects in
Science and Prospects in Social Development." My instructions were "to
give the audience a studied view of possible social and economic developments which will, inevitably, have impact upon the financial and other
entities which CPAs serve."

Despite the fact that I work at The RAND Corporation, that I have
written about the social and political implications of new science and
technology, that by coincidence I live on a street called Oracle Place
and that we inherited a dog already named Cassandra - despite all that -
I shall not give you a long list of prophecies, forecasts, predictions or
guesses about the "future" into which you can fit your professional role
or to which you might passively try to accommodate yourselves. I hope
that my necessarily sketchy remarks will make clear why I have rejected
this opportunity to become known to you as a man of "imagination" by
startling you with dramatic scenarios of things to come. There are many
kinds of projections developed for various purposes by various people.
Some are important intellectual tools whose users are aware of the limited purposes to be served by models of future states of affairs. And
there is a lot of crystal ball gazing as a means to mobilize public concern, or to shock or to entertain. But there is no time here for a presumably learned critique of forecasting technique.

Instead, I shall offer some thoughts about how to think about the
future.

Let's start with the theme developed by Dennis Gabor in his stimulating book *Inventing the Future*:

"The future cannot be predicted, but futures can be invented. It
was man's ability to invent which has made human society what it is. The
mental processes of inventions are still mysterious. They are rational
but not logical, that is to say, not deductive. The first step of the
technological or social inventor is to visualize by an act of imagination
a thing or state of things which does not yet exist and which to him appears in some ways desirable. He can then start rationally arguing back-

---

* This paper was prepared for presentation at the 80th Annual Meeting of the American Institute of Certified Public Accountants held in
Portland, Oregon, September 27, 1967.

wards from the invention and forward from the means at his disposal until
a way is found from one to the other."*

I would argue for the following propositions:

1. *"The future"* is not pre-ordained and therefore it cannot and
will not be "discovered"by any individual genius or massive Manhattan
District research project. If "it" were knowable or became known in that
sense, our whole conception of human life would be fantastically different and incomprehensible to us sitting here.

2. On the other hand, the future is not a blank void within which
anything and everything is equally possible or likely.

3. The future, like the past and the present, is essentially man-
made. There is a physical world and there is nature but even these are
being deliberately and inadvertantly subjected to human management - and
mismanagement.

4. What man does, what he dreams, what he thinks, what he con-
ciously and unconsciously remembers has constituted the past, accounts
for the present and will shape the future. The ability to communicate
and to modify his own and other people's behavior based on language, mem-
ory and experience are what differentiates us from animals, minerals and
vegetables. There are known or knowable connections between our present
but changing perceptions of the past, and these reach out with broad continuities into the future.

5. Because of these continuities, it should be easier to describe
"the future" in an aggregate sense that it is to predict discrete technological inventions or to predict in the social world sudden discontinuities, abrupt accelerations or declines in rates of change - especially
if you also want to specify the dates, the probabilities and the magni-
tudes.

6. I have talked about "the future" in quotation marks because man
is already creating much of it. Much of "it" is here, perhaps in undra-
matic or in small-scale outline. And what our many futures will be like
in 1984 or by the year 2000, depends to a challenging extent on what we
make it by design, by action and by inaction. Or to put it another way,
to plan better to solve our present problems will make a significant dent
on what the future will be like.

7. I don't believe that there is necessarily or need be a fundamental conflict or contradiction between our democratic and humanistic values
and "inventing" our futures. This depends on the kind of future goals we
want to achieve. As we shall see later, the choice of goals, the values
we seek to enhance and the means to such ends are difficult to decide.
In fact the process of goal clarification, of the values to be sought and
the assessment of means appropriate to such ends is what inventing the
future is, or should be, all about. That is what the task is if we are
not fatalists.

I would view as fatalists those who are super-optimists - those who
think that the lesser the amount of planning the greater the odds for the
system to produce optimal results. And there are also the fatalistic
pessimists who are convinced that mankind doesn't have what it takes and
that all his efforts at self-betterment are illusory and doomed to disap-
pointment if not extinction. I'm not sure how to classify the man who
says he is an optimist because he believes the future is uncertain.

---

* Dennis Gabor, *Inventing the Future,* pp. 207-208, New York, 1964.

8. Finally, I believe that an effort to solve presently visible future problems is worthwhile in itself, even if in fact those efforts don't
result in the hoped for solution. In fact, it would be most unlikely
that the results will ever turn out without surprises, but my contention
is that the exercise of planning for the future will compel us to acquire
better knowledge about present problems and how to cope with them.

* * *

In the past ten years several dozen scholarly institutes and centers
have been created, here and aborad, which claim the future as their focus.
By now almost every large business, government agency and professional
society, including your own, has a long range planning group.

Why this interest in the future - and not just interest in it but
anxiety about it?

I think it mirrors the shaken confidence of the capitalist world,
particularly in the United States, in the inevitability of progress as it
has defined the term since the period of the Enlightenment and the Industrial Revolution. In America, to oversimplify it, we had confidence that
the basic rules of the game provided a structure within which all would
work out for the best. The main requirement was to minimize the planning
function of free government, and to protect free market mechanisms and
decentralized institutions.

The impressive record of stable government under the social invention called the U.S. Constitution and the success of the U.S. economic
system built upon the virtues and values of the Christian ethic, seemed
to justify strong faith that all would work out for the best in this the
best country if not the best of all possible worlds. The hostility to
social planning for the future, at least as an emotional attitude if not
in practice, was and to some extent still is testimony to the faith in a
benevolent future if we don't tamper too much with the present.

At the same time, Americans have another strong set of beliefs: your
individual future is what you want to make it and what you plan to make
it. The absence of a feudal history; the role of the frontier and a
richly endowed continent to populate and develop; the freedoms assured by
our political, legal and economic systems; the absence of fixed class and
caste lines - all made for a faith in individual planning: pick your future, study and work, evaluate your choices and decisions in terms of
their pragmatic effect in moving you to your goal - and your chance of
achieving it is very good. And in fact if each person plans well for
achieving his self-chosen private future, society itself would benefit
and progress achieved. But keep the planning to the immediate self or to
one's immediate family, group or business. If the planning is done by
large institutions - large corporations, or unions or government bodies,
that's bad.

But many things happened in the past fifty years to shake national
confidence in the semi-automatic yet self-propelled road to progress,
success, happiness: the succession of world wars and lesser wars since
1914, the great depression and the anxiety about the economy even when
booming were primary faith shakers. Public opinion, despite vigorous
opposition, turned to larger institutions to manage things more directly
- to preserve peace, to insure domestic tranquility and to regulate the
economy - hopefully to create or re-establish an environment which would

still foster the real engines of progress - the individual pursuit of
personal goals.

My thesis is not that the trend toward what I'll call social planning to distinguish personal and individual planning, has been necessarily
good or bad, well done or poorly done - but first to establish that this
country has lived from the beginning in a social environment where at the
same time planning has been both active and accepted (an anti-fatalist
view at the individual or selective group level), and opposed for larger
political, economic and social institutions, with a fatalistic certitude
that only individual planning will ensure progress.

How does all this square with current interest in "The Future," including the inclusion on the program of this professional society of a
half day session devoted to anticipating the future?

As with many other groups and individuals, your confidence has in
fact been shaken that all that you do in a short time perspective - day
by day or even year by year - will automatically or necessarily be for
the best ten or 25 years from now. You probably feel, as does any pro-
gress-striving group, that if only you could get a pretty good preview of
the future, you could do a better job here and now in achieving your
present set of goals for progress and success at a later date. In principle that is fine. In fact, there are many pitfalls - depending on how
you conceive of the problem of forecasting, prediction, prevision, fore-
sight, planning and purposes. And all of us are aware that our private
pursuits are now more closely linked to larger segments of society - not
just to family, business or profession, but to the city, the country, the
world.

Anyone's preview inventory of America's future social environment
probably would resemble an inventory of our current concerns. What we do
about them now or fail to do, mainly will determine how these issues will
characterize what the next generation will experience as its present. I
say "mainly determine" because there is always a probability that some
currently unforeseeable developments will occur with some startling and
abrupt consequence. But such discontinuities are as unpredictable as is
a "break-through" in a field of science.

What are some of the problem issues which integrally link the present to the future?

My check-list includes at least these gross categories, each of
which splinters into innumerable specifics yet all of which interact in
most complex and imperfectly understood ways.

. World peace and international relations

. Economic growth and stability

. Population: growth rates, composition, geography

. Government operation and organization at all levels

. Technological change: including problem-solving "systems" along
with the hardware

. Economic organization: the role of the corporation, private business large and small, Uncle Sam as largest customer, organized labor, the
work force, automation, economic growth and stability

. Urban affairs: pollution, transportation, race relations, ghettos,
delinquency, crime, drugs

. General welfare: physical and mental health, leisure, education, information

. "Quality of life": the family and the generations, the sense of personal responsibility and conscience, implicit ethical norms, respect for self and for others, the dimensions of privacy.

Obviously I cannot review here the present state of knowledge on any of these areas or extrapolate from such knowledge into the future or suggest preferred "solutions." But I shall offer a few observations of general pertinence to them all.

Better understanding of current conditions entails many things.

A first requirement is better diagnosis. This requires in the longer run a more rapid development of the social sciences and social scientists, including such practitioners as lawyers, public officials and administrators. It means not only specialists but also more and better generalists who by training and diversified experience develop insight into the many interconnections between the proliferating specialists and specialties.

This need for better diagnosis is getting increased attention, not only in the universities where it is a central, centuries-old tradition, but in government and business as well. What is new is an updating of data, a search for hitherto neglected aspects of the problem, refinements in analytical methods and a closer relation between research, policy and action.

Also there seems to be a heightened awareness by planners and researchers of the dangers of hidden and subtle bias in the way of a problem is posed. Such biases may stem from the class, profession or psychological background of the analyst and express itself not only in formulation of the problem but in research design, or in the lumping together of seemingly similar factors which in fact conceal important interrelations. There is more awareness today I believe among planners that value preferences need to be laid bare and implicit assumptions be disclosed. One of the most difficult tasks in planning for future development is not only to establish the present preferences, value systems and objectives of differential groups but to understand how these may change and to allow for the likelihood that what we think is wanted or desired today may not in fact be so preferred in the future.

As an example, take the history of many urban renewal and slum clearance programs. Obviously they have not provided better housing for the slum-dweller nor have slum-dwellers who were reinstalled in more hygienic low cost housing projects been unambivalently happy about it. Why? Because left out of the physical rehabilitation was a human conception of what mattered greatly to the people - a sense of neighborhood, a community of easy social contact, a place of life as well as a place to live.

Or take many of the badly understood dimensions of the negro-white problem despite a vast body of important sociological research during the past half-century. It is often believed that discrimination and job opportunities for negroes are most troublesome for the unskilled and those who are high school dropouts. A more careful gathering and analysis of statistical data now suggests that employment difficulties are relatively greater for negroes who are high school graduates and who have had some college education. This seemingly simple re-analysis suggests some modi-

fication in current programs, and their "target" choices, and thus in efforts to ameliorate some future problems.

Probably all of you have heard in recent years of "systems analysis"
and PPBS: Program Planning Budgeting System as developed by my colleagues
at The RAND Corporation, by other researchers, introduced in the Department of Defense in 1961 and by direction of the President two years ago
to be employed by all federal agencies in managing and planning their future operations. There is little doubt that the extension of PPBS will
of itself have considerable effect on future ways of solving problems,
managing organizations and intensifying the trend toward social planning
- all of this with what is essentially an old common-sensical idea.

The essence of PPBS, although complex in the doing, is simple: to
relate the resources one plans to expend to the accomplishments or outcomes of that expenditure. Or to put it another way, it is a way of sys-
tematically weighing my choices in advance by thinking through alternative
goals, objectives and programs, in relation to the comparative benefits
from alternative paths to such goals - and in relation to realistically
estimated costs associated with each.

In social development, "costs" and "benefits" are not adequately
measured by such manageable criteria as dollars or units of output. If
there is a future for such planning strategies, several intellectual
problems have to be solved.

The first I have alluded to: the need for far more detailed understanding of what a given organization, agency or social problem now consists of, what is it, how did it get that way, what preferences, purposes, goals is it advancing or inhibiting. Where dollar profits and
losses are not the pay-off, such as what constitutes decent health and
social welfare of the aged, it is incredibly difficult to relate dollars
expended to results achieved, and thus, to relate sensibly means to ends.

Many of our major national and local efforts proceed, in great earn-
estness and sincerity, knowing neither what the programs are expected to
accomplish, especially for the intended beneficiaries, nor how to evaluate the consequences in order to modify programs, or goals, or both.
Witness the frustration of Detroit and New Haven, to name but two battlegrounds of 1967. Housing projects, slum clearance, job training programs,
community participation roles shared by negroes - all presumably had been
tried, but the ghettos erupted nonetheless. In fact, have such programs
failed because, like Christianity, they were in fact too little tried?
Or do such programs make utterly erroneous assumptions about the deeper
psychological, social and political values and attitudes of lower class
negroes? Who really knows? I daresay that the gap in communication is
enormous between slum-roots negro and social agencies. The lack of match
is cavernous between the values and deep inner needs of slum negroes and
how these are perceived by whites who are truly eager to promote social
development and who do the planning. And apparently even those negroes
who have made it by the standards of successful middle class America are
out of touch with the seething resentments of the ghetto masses.

I don't know for certain, but I have a hunch that the leaders of
"black power," whatever their private motives, have come closer to the
jugular: the craving of a down-trodden minority for self-respect built
upon self-accomplishment. However demagogic the language or platforms of
"black power," it does seem to have a better insight into the need to repair the damaged sense of self-esteem among many negroes than do the well-

meaning conscience-stricken and necessarily paternalistic white Establishments. Until our national and local programs better understand and take into account the emotional make-up and value systems of the urban negro, we won't make much direct headway in reducing the problems of race for the future.

The inadequacy of basic social data and the need for more sophisticated analyses of it has become recognized increasingly not just by scholars but by those trying to change the present to make a better future. The realization is growing that the preferred American style of act first, think second, may not quite suffice in solving big problems for the future. Dozens of programs have been hastily planned, budgeted and adopted in recent years. I do not in this context challenge their purposes nor their need. Many were long and shamefully overdue. But we come to the reckoning. Doubt has grown whether their purposes were adequately defined and consonant with the means established for their accomplishment. I say "doubt" because we don't adequately know what has been achieved, for whom, at what human and other costs with what longer-term implications.

A bill is pending before the Senate, introduced by Senator Walter Mondale of Minnesota, to develop the kinds of data needed for more rational social development and planning by the decision-makers, private as well as public, at federal, state and local community levels. The proposal is to have a counterpart to the President's Council of Economic Advisors which reports on economic developments - a Council of Social Advisors, who will reorganize and develop information systems labeled "Social Indicators" from which reports on the social health of the country can be prepared. Social audits and social accounting are visible needs and in principle represent concepts analogous to your own professional auditing functions. I need not detail the innumerable issues of method and quality which will plague the field of social auditing. There will be good and poorly conceived and performed audits as there are in financial accounting operations, but I am sure that the scale of such ventures in applied social science will be vastly increased over past and present efforts. Hopefully, a better social knowledge will further social development at least in two ways:

- To identify things we are now doing which upon awareness we decide we ought to stop doing in order to survive, or to have lives worth living; and

- To help think through some of the things we may want to consider doing and to assess in advance the likely consequences of pursuing one or another course of action.

I don't want to leave you with the impression that I have a zealot's faith in science - that science or social science can save us, if given the resources. Nor do I minimize for the future as I do not do for the past the role of chance, of individual impact on social developments, on politics, on cultural accomplishment. In fact, a prime goal for planning, in my view, and a prime criterion for assessing its quality, is the extent to which individual differences and opportunities are nurtured, pluralism of ideas and institutions are fostered and opportunities for self-chosen paths of fulfillment are widened. In short, freedom and future planning can and should be mutually supporting.

I don't expect the future necessarily to have any less tension than has been part of our past. No dynamic society is tension- or trouble-free. Only static societies think they are calm, but they too have their

outlets in suicide, alcoholism and other ways. I think we shall find, as
we already can see, that economic affluence alone is not a "cure." To
work on a larger scale to remedy social ills also creates heightened expectations which rarely are met. There will be less tolerance of traditional authority in the family, in the larger community, in the here-
after. The sense of what constitutes a fair share of income, health,
education, respect and political power will be perhaps even more contro-
versial than at present. And the resulting tensions will themselves be
part of the problem and the efforts at solution. The changers and the
resisters of change will have new battlegrounds over new issues and new
ideas and these need to be reflected among the costs and benefits in construction of social balance sheets.

* * *

Let me conclude by briefly mentioning a few things I would urge you
to do apart from perhaps pondering what has already been said. There are
things you can do in your role as citizen and as responsible policy advisors.

First, don't sit on your *status quo* by leaving social development to
those whose job description so prescribes.

Don't just moan and groan about those bureaucrats, those professors,
those politicians. Their problems are yours, and more yours than the
mass population's.

Don't underestimate either your potential influence, affluence or
intelligence by taking your marbles out of the game.

No one has a monopoly on ideas, least of all people in government.
I should think that the financial and tax stake that you have in urban
America would compel you to make the urban problem a challenge to private
business. I should think that you could accumulate the resources to analyze in detail your city's problems and develop combined public-private
programs which would pay off in more ways than one.

Let me give an earlier example of one possible approach. Some of
you may be members of a remarkably foresighted organization of businessmen who during World War II went about the task, independent of government, of preventing and inventing an important part of their future.
They organized the Committee for Economic Development to study the problem of postwar industrial conversion to a peacetime economy. They anticipated the possibilities of depression. They worked along with tal-
ented scholars to study these possibilities and to develop policies which
would prevent the crises which seemed likely. And they made an important
impact on their future.

Some of you in this professional society might right now form a Committee on Social Development - not just a discussion body but a serious
working group, teamed up with carefully chosen professional research
staffs, to compete with public planning groups in the search for better
futures. Surely you have the self-confidence to permit such a Committee
for Social Development to function in an objective non-trade association
manner and thus to attract outstanding talent, nationally and in regional
branches.

For members of the financial accounting community to participate in a serious effort at social accounting would put yourselves into the business of acting constructively on the future instead of nervously trying to anticipate and to adjust to a world you never made. For if too many people of your stature pull out, you and the rest of us will have a marvelous future - behind us.

An unfortunately all-too-common viewpoint is
that the future is the concern only of the
futurists, that is, only of the professional
forecasters and planners. In the concluding
essay, Dr. Waskow argues that this is an erroneous viewpoint. It is bad enough if the
futurists believe this, but it would be a
tragedy if the rest of the people believed
it, and decided that the future could be left
to the futurists. His suggestions for involving non-futurists in the study of the future
deserve careful attention.

FUTURISM: ELITIST OR DEMOCRATIC?*

ARTHUR I. WASKOW
Institute for Policy Studies, Washington, D.C., U.S.A.

Taking their cues from a few avant-garde experiments in Europe, a
number of well-established American institutions have during the last
five years fostered the creation of a whole new "profession": The study
of the future.

For example, in 1965 the American Academy of Arts and Sciences ap-
pointed a Commission on the Year 2000, headed by Daniel Bell of Columbia
University. The commission set the tone for most of the new profession
by regarding itself as a panel of the priesthood, to whom the mysteries
were revealed and who could guide the people but would not open those
mysteries to the people. (When one commission member proposed inviting a
number of young people to join it on the grounds that they might actually
live till the year 2000 and might already be carrying the attitudes that
would deeply affect the history of that year, he was told that mere youth
could not make them experts - and only experts could do the requisite
planning.)

Similarly, in Rand Corp., there has grown out of concern with the
future of military strategy a group with a wider interest in the future
of American policy generally; but that interest remains oriented to the
group of people that runs the Government of the United States and is still
based on the assumption that this need not, could not, ought not, be in
any sense the property of the American public. (The Rand group helped
bring into being an Institute for the Future which will open its doors
within the year, on a Carnegie grant.)

The new elite futurologists deny that elitism is a problem at all,
saying that just as astronomy is a matter for the professional, so the
study of the future must be. They hand down their "findings" to the
public through books, pamphlets, conferences, etc. Usually they take
the "public" to mean a slightly larger circle of experts, administrators,
businessmen and politicians.

ANGRY CHALLENGE

When one such effort at dissemination - a convocation called earlier
this year by the Foreign Policy Association - tried to invite the young
to attend and listen but not to speak, such elite futurologists as Bell
and Emmanuel Mesthene of Harvard were not even able to understand the bite

*From: *The Wall Street Journal*, 12 Sept., 1968.

and anger of the challenge put by a number of young liberals and radicals:
"Is the future indeed a subject like astronomy, or does it belong to
all the people - who should therefore understand and decide it? Why
should only 'future leaders' be involved in imagining the future, rather
than the schoolteachers, welfare mothers, auto workers, stock brokers,
shopkeepers and high school dropouts who will make up the future?"

What the dissidents at the FPA's convocation were saying was a 21st
century version of that old saw, "Knowledge is power." In a super-industrial society, knowledge of the future is enormous power, and ignorance
of the future may prevent the powerless from feeling revulsion and anger
until it is too late. Decisions on research and development of weapon
systems made today will affect what the world looks like 20 years from
now. They will affect, for example, whether it is even *possible* to
achieve a disarmed world 20 years hence. Decisions on seemingly less
crucial matters like the supersonic transport will affect the way our
cities develop 10 years hence. Very few people know this - only the experts with an "interest" in the matter, an established political or economic interest that they already know about.

The rest of the public is not ready to worry, not trained to worry;
it won't get angry about sonic booms till the SSTs are already there, and
that will be too late. In an era of very swift technological change, it
has to be possible for the whole public to be able to understand the possible futures confronting their society 20, 25, 30 years from now, in
order to be able to insist on the decisions to be made now that would enable the kind of society they want to emerge 20 or 30 years from now.

In response to these conflicting values and interests of the public
and private good, there have emerged various and conflicting styles of
futurism. At the First International Future Research Congress, held last
September in Oslo, the futurists divided into three groups. One might be
called the techno-planners - concerned chiefly with technological forecasting. They had frequently been involved in systems-analysis kinds of
work. They saw the future as buildable through governments and similar
large-scale institutions with very considerable power. Most of them were
from the United States, many from Rand Corp. or similar institutions.
They put forward their images of how one might construct pieces of the
21st century, and described ways in which they have worked with governments in the super-industrial or in the underdeveloped world, to try to
construct those pieces. For them, "planning" was clearly a way of help-
ing those who now hold power to know what they must do to keep holding
power 30 or 50 years hence. What must they change, where should they beat
a strategic retreat, what new organizations and technologies should they
invent, when can they hold the line?

The second major group at Oslo might be called the humanist social
democrats. They included most of the Europeans, both Eastern and Western,
plus a couple of Americans. They were typically in their mid-50s, about
a decade older than the techno-planners. They were quite distressed at
technocratic planning. The Eastern Europeans tended to be very critical
of the way central planning had operated in Eastern Europe from 1946 or
'47 until fairly recently; and were concerned about the ignoring of human
values that had resulted from pressure from a central planning source for
technological advance and swift economic development. They tended to see
the Western, especially American, technocrats as quite similar to the
state planners with whom they'd had to cope in Poland and Czechoslovakia.
And they feared that human values would similarly get lost. There was

considerable horror, for example, over an attempt to plan a 700-million-person megalopolis on the Bay of Bengal for the middle of the 21st century - the second group feeling horrified that this could not possibly be a *human* social system and that planning it and getting the Indian government to begin building it was the same kind of process that they had gone through in Eastern Europe. They were frightened of that, and most of the Western Europeans agreed with them.

In reaction against the "expert" orientation of the elitist technological planners, the social democrats at their best have tried to move one step beyond "planning" toward teaching the general public the art of thinking in a 30 to 40 year span. For example, the discussions of the "Mankind 2000" project, involving an international group of scholars, centering in Western Europe and Britain but including some Americans and East Europeans, have focused on how to involve large numbers of the public in planning the future. Robert Jungk of the Mankind 2000 group has suggested a permanent (perhaps mobile) exposition of the future, in which larger numbers of visitors than those usually oriented to books would be exposed to vivid exhibitions of the possible social realities of the future. Charles Osgood of the Mankind 2000 group is exploring, through Project Plato at the University of Illinois, the possibilities of using computer and teaching-machine technology to make available complex sets of branching choices, leading to various futures, so that participants could play through certain choices in the present to see how they might open up and close off various possible futures.

LITTLE ROOM FOR INVENTION

Both of these experimental efforts move in the direction of involving large sections of the public in future-thinking, but both still present the public with *faits accomplis* and leave little room for the invention of new forms or parts of the future, on the local and personal levels, that would mesh with large-scale change and make it viable.

Finally, there was at Oslo a third group, made up of several young North Americans, a couple of Englishmen and some Scandinavians - typically in their early thirties. They might be called the participatory futurists. They were equally distressed by top-down technocratic planning and by what many of them felt was a kind of literary fuzziness in the humanist social democrats. They criticized the social democrats from the standpoint that they were not able to make anything real out of their fears or their hopes, and that the literary and philosophical musings with which they seemed to confront topdown planning, whether the Eastern or Western variety, was not an effective way of building the kind of future which they seemed to want to build.

The typical methodology of this third group could be called one of "creative disorder": Attempting to project a decent and workable vision of the future over a one-generation-hence time period, and then attempting to build chunks of that future in the present. But not to build them with the help of presently powerful institutions; to build them from the bottom, without the permission of the powerful, and often against the laws or the mores of the present "order."

Some of the participatory futurists were working on such unorthodox projects, intended to represent chunks of a possible future, as neighborhood-level quasi-governments in metropolitan centers - democratically run and oriented partly to such traditional issues as schools or housing but

also involved in imagining alternative futures for the neighborhood.
Others at Oslo were working to put together transnational groups of
scholars and students interested in projecting visions of world order -
which those groups of people, by their very existence and action as transnational bodies, would help to bring into existence.

And the methodology in this third group was, therefore, quite different from the methodology of both of the first two. They did not tend
to do any technological forecasting; most of them were not technologically
trained; and they were deeply skeptical about involvement with governments
as the way of bringing about a decent future.

EXAMPLES FROM AMERICA

Not only the Americans among the participatory futurists, but also
some of the Europeans, were influenced by ways in which some American social movements of the '60s had turned images of the future into potent
political action in the present. The neatest case is the sit-ins, where
the civil rights movement said:

"Our desirable-achievable future is that we want to be able to eat in
integrated restaurants. We will not petition legislatures to require integration, we will not petition the owners of the restaurants to integrate, we will simply create the future. That is, we will integrate the
restaurants, and it will rest upon those who have the power of law and
the power of ownership in their hands to decide how to respond to that
creation. So we will build now what it is we want to exist in the future,
and the powerful will have to react to that. They will have to let us
build it, or punish us for trying. If they punish us, we believe we can
build support around that vision of the future, and can therefore mobilize
even more people into action to achieve it."

All these efforts assume the creation of strains and tensions between
the imagined future and the existing present. Creating and judging the
strain is crucial, in order for the "piece of the future" to be neither
smashed nor ignored, but create enough change to move the society. That
is creative disorder: Disorder because it obeys the "law and order" of
some more or less distant future, and is therefore likely to be "un-
lawful" or "disorderly" by the standards of the present.

One who uses this approach should not expect that his picture of the
future will be achieved. He must expect exactly the opposite, that along
the way the process of imagination and creation will lead him to change
his own imagination, and that by engaging wholly new people in imagining
the future who do not now imagine it, the process will help them create
a kind of future that he did not imagine when he began.

Thus the participatory futurist begins with a mythical vision, a pro-
visional vision, of the future as an open-ended future; a future free to
decide on its own future; a society in which politics can happen, in
which different groups of people are able to press toward change in the
society.

INDEX